OS
635.9772
SQU

B⁴⁰

ADB-
1240

Check Out Receipt

Branciforte

23- 6/13

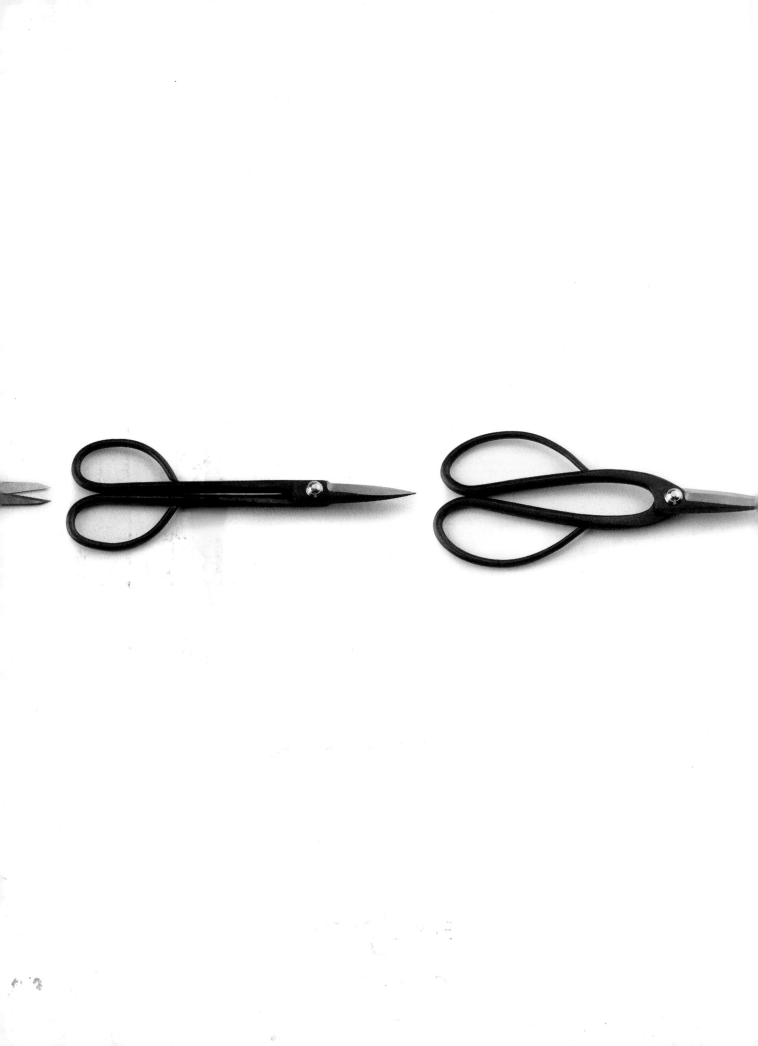

Successful
Bonsai

Raising Exotic Miniature Trees

David Squire

FIREFLY BOOKS

A FIREFLY BOOK

Published by Firefly Books Ltd. 2006

Copyright © 2006 New Holland Publishers (U.K.) Ltd.
Text copyright © 2006 David Squire
Illustrations copyright © 2006 Louwra Marais
Photographs copyright © 2006 André Wepener from Digital Images
Solutions (except as noted on p157)

First printing

Publisher Cataloging-in-Publication Data (U.S)

Squire, David., 1938-
   Successful bonsai : raising exotic miniature trees / David Squire.
[158] p. : col. ill. ; cm.
Includes index.
Summary: A guide to raising exotic miniature trees in both indoor
and outdoor settings. Includes an A–Z reference of 80 indoor and 15
classical species.
ISBN 1-55407-157-7 (pbk.)
1. Bonsai. I. Title.
635.9/772 dc22 SB433.5.S63 2006

Library and Archives Canada Cataloguing in Publication

Squire, David
   Successful bonsai : raising exotic miniature trees / David Squire.
Includes index.
ISBN 1-55407-157-7
1. Bonsai. I. Title.
SB433.5.S63 2006   635.9'772   C2005-905054-3

Published in the United States by
Firefly Books (U.S.) Inc.
P.O. Box 1338, Ellicott Station
Buffalo, New York 14205

Published in Canada by
Firefly Books Ltd.
66 Leek Crescent
Richmond Hill, Ontario L4B 1H1

ISBN 13: 978-155407-157-9

Printed in Malaysia

Contents

Wild Olive (Olea europaea *sp.* africana)
(Artist: Rudi Adam)

Introduction

Growing bonsai is an all-consuming hobby and one that will enthrall you with its techniques and artistry. Traditional bonsai is the practice of growing miniature hardy trees, shrubs and conifers in containers outdoors in temperate areas according to time-honored Chinese and Japanese customs, whereas indoor bonsai is concerned with growing tropical and subtropical shrubs and trees indoors, again mainly in temperate climates but also in warm and colder areas.

Traditional bonsai can be traced back 1,000 or more years to China, while there are claims that a form of growing miniature trees was known much earlier in India. Whatever its true origin, traditional bonsai has come to be associated with religious thoughts and naturalism, as well as with the concept that mountains, trees and rocks have a soul. Some bonsai historians even suggest that the gnarled and contorted shapes of the miniature trees represent the bodies of the immortal in the next world.

About 1,200 years ago the Japanese absorbed bonsai into their culture, where it was perfected into an art steeped in beauty and correctness. It is this preciseness of purpose, and desire for perfection in mirroring nature, that has encapsulated the soul of bonsai. Incidentally, the term bonsai is derived from *bon-sai*; *bon* being the Japanese word for "tray", while *sai* translates as "planting". The word "bonsai" is both singular and plural in its usage.

Opposite: *Traditional bonsai are kept outdoors throughout the year, with only brief visits indoors to display their flowers. Indoor bonsai, however, are houseplants, only temporarily put outside in temperate climates during summer.*

The history of bonsai

For many centuries, the Japanese refined the techniques of the art of bonsai to a point where an aged specimen was considered to be a prized family heirloom. Bonsai was little known in the West before the beginning of the 20th century. In 1909, however, an exhibition of bonsai was held in London, England, where it caused a sensation. The art of bonsai was, as a result, taken up by many people throughout the world and is today a keenly followed facet of gardening and cultivating plants.

Indoor bonsai – the creation of miniature plants in small containers by using tropical and subtropical plants – is a relatively new concept and, at first, was not accepted by traditional bonsai enthusiasts as they believed it did not reflect the true spirit of bonsai. Nevertheless, indoor bonsai has advanced, enriched and enlarged the original concept of the art, making it possible for many more people to grow miniaturized plants.

actinophylla (Australian ivy palm). In the mid-1970s, the Brooklyn Botanic Garden in New York state published a book about indoor bonsai following a widely praised and acclaimed display of these plants.

City dwellers without gardens were especially enthusiastic about growing bonsai indoors. Unlike traditional bonsai, which in temperate regions are outdoor plants, tropical and subtropical plants are able to survive central heating.

Thirty or more years later, enthusiasm for indoor bonsai has spread to many countries and added to the wealth of plants that can be grown indoors. Traditional bonsai enthusiasts were initially scathing of this new concept, but most are now embracing it with the enthusiasm it deserves.

Where did indoor bonsai originate?

Pinpointing the exact place and time when indoor bonsai originated is not easy. It is certain, however, that many enthusiasts of traditional bonsai sometimes took these plants indoors for limited periods.

Indoor bonsai began when someone in a temperate climate pruned and remodelled a tropical or subtropical houseplant, such as the *Ficus benjamina* (Java fig – occasionally also known as weeping fig), *Malpighia coccigera* (Singapore holly) or *Schefflera*

Opposite: *The art of bonsai, depicted in many Japanese paintings and drawings, reveals the influence of miniature plants in homes as well as within society. They were the focus of conversation, as well as family activities.*
Right: *Often, enthusiasm for indoor bonsai begins when a plant is received as a present. It is then that contact should be made with a specialist nursery to see what plants are available and the styles that capture your attention and to seek advice on how to create these miniature shrubs, trees and conifers.*

How do indoor bonsai differ from outdoor bonsai?

The major difference between an indoor bonsai and a traditional bonsai is that the traditional type is hardy outdoors in winter in temperate climates, while the indoor trees are tropical and subtropical and need warmth during winter — although some can stand outdoors in summer if the weather is warm.

The techniques of pruning and training both these types of bonsai are similar, but whereas the growth of traditional bonsai is strongly influenced by the changing seasons, indoor bonsai often have a continuous growing period, although their growth is more active in spring and summer than in winter.

As much care needs to be invested in choosing and buying an indoor bonsai as an outdoor bonsai but, because many of the species for indoor bonsai are also grown as houseplants, there is greater opportunity to buy and modify a plant. This can be an inexpensive way to start — as well as to expand — an indoor-bonsai collection. The styles in which plants can be trained are mainly the same for both types of bonsai.

The growth of traditional bonsai is significantly influenced and regulated by the changing seasons and invariably by harmonious temperatures and light intensities. A temperature rise in spring, for example, is balanced by a higher light intensity. Indoor bonsai, on the other hand, are often exposed to an imbalance of high temperatures and little light in winter. Plants can be selected to survive these conditions, but another solution is to provide growth-inducing light (*see* p. 78). As well as encouraging healthy growth, this illumination highlights indoor bonsai and makes them more distinctive as room features.

Whether you are progressing from outdoor to indoor bonsai, or from houseplants to indoor bonsai, you will be captivated by these plants that will enrich your life as well as bring great vitality and interest to your home.

Opposite: *An indoor bonsai is given diffused light during summer to protect its flowers and young leaves from strong sunlight. In winter, shading is not usually necessary, but be guided by the intensity of the light.*

Chapter 1

Buying and propagating indoor bonsai

There are several sources of established indoor bonsai, including specialist bonsai nurseries and garden centers. It is also possible to buy a young, healthy houseplant, radically prune it and repot it into a bonsai container.

Often, enthusiasm for indoor bonsai begins when a plant is received as a present. At that stage it is worth contacting a specialist bonsai nursery to see the wide range of plants that are available. Bonsai are usually kept in a display area, but you might also be able to see them in a "growing" area for "small" plants. Many indoor bonsai enthusiasts decide to grow their own plants from seeds or, usually, cuttings. Clearly, it takes several years to produce an indoor bonsai from seeds and cuttings, but patience is repaid by the creation of a plant grown solely through your own endeavor.

Opposite: *Young bonsai plants growing in a specialist nursery.*

Display areas in bonsai nurseries invariably have plants arranged on tiered benches. This allows prospective buyers to inspect them and also ensures good air circulation and plenty of sunlight. The trees are probably all superb examples, but there usually is one that captures your attention through its unusual shape, or especially attractive leaves and flowers.

Sourcing your bonsai

There are a number of ways to start a collection of indoor bonsai:

Specialist nurseries

A reputable nursery is an ideal place to buy an indoor bonsai. You will also be able to get first-hand information about the potting mix in which it is growing and when it should be repotted next.

Garden centers

Usually, these sources of indoor bonsai are acceptable, but information about individual plants may not be as good as that from a specialist nursery. Additionally, ask for confirmation that the bonsai has not recently been transformed from a house-

plant; such plant conversions are fine, but not if you are paying "established bonsai" prices.

Modifying houseplants

Young, healthy houseplants can be converted into indoor bonsai, and are an inexpensive way to start your collection. Further information on this is provided on pp. 28–35.

Raising your own plants

If you have a greenhouse, or solarium or sunroom, raising your own plants is an inexpensive way to start a collection. (*See* pp. 25–27 for details on how to propagate plants.)

What to look for when buying an indoor bonsai

For long-term success, always begin with a healthy plant. Following are guidelines on how to judge whether a plant is healthy:

Leaves

These should be bright green, without any signs of damage from pests and diseases (*see* pp. 80–87). Check surfaces of the leaves.

Buds and shoots

Buds should be fresh and undamaged, with firm, young shoots. Avoid plants that are growing close together, as this sometimes damages the shoots. Dried, shrunken buds indicate watering has been neglected.

Bonsai trained in a cascade style, like the one shown here, always capture attention. Before buying a bonsai, check that it is healthy and that its shape reflects the style you are trying to achieve.

Trunk and branches

Depending on the style, bonsai trunks can be upright, leaning or cascading, but whatever their nature, they must be strong and healthy, as well as elegant and tapering. Their apexes must give the impression of being natural and free from excessive manipulation. Additionally, on upright and slanting (leaning) styles, the lowest branches should be the largest and most dominant, and positioned about one-third of the way up the trunks. Aesthetically, the inter-branch areas should have a sense of space, and enable light and air to circulate around the branches. Check crevices on the trunk and branches for signs of pests and diseases.

Container and root ball

The container should be either distinctly shallow, or deep and upright, with no noticeable cracks or chips. The container should not dominate the bonsai and its length should be between two-thirds to three-quarters of the tree's height. Additionally, the depth of the container should be approximately the same as the diameter of the trunk near its base, with the exception of cascading bonsai, which have deeper containers.

Roots climbing out of the container from between the edges of the potting mix and container indicate that repotting has not been maintained, while dirty containers are a sign of general neglect.

Proportion and style

As well as inspecting the plant and container, check the position of the bonsai. For example, in an oval or rectangular container, the bonsai is best positioned about one-third of the pot's length from one of the ends. For most styles the bonsai is aligned centrally along the container's length. The size, shape and color of the container must harmonize with the bonsai (colors and shapes of containers are described on pp. 57–60).

Getting your bonsai home

Established indoor bonsai are usually fairly expensive and therefore care is essential when transporting them home.

When using a car:

* Do not position the bonsai in strong sunlight or near a draft from an open window.
* Slow down for speed bumps and potholes.
* It may also be best to leave young children and dogs at home.

Raising new plants

Raising your own plants is one of the most inspirational and satisfying parts of gardening, and with a few pieces of equipment it is possible to produce plants suitable for indoor bonsai. Taking cuttings and sowing seeds are the easiest ways to increase plants.

Air layering (*see* glossary, p.149) is possible on several indoor plants and often associated with *Ficus elastica* (rubber plant), a popular houseplant. It has large leaves, however, and is unsuitable as an indoor bonsai.

Increasing plants from seeds

Seeds of many plants that can be propagated as indoor bonsai are widely available from most seed companies and specialist bonsai nurseries. They include flowering and foliage plants, such as:

* *Camellia japonica* (common camellia) (*see* p. 95)
* X *Citrofortunella microcarpa*, syn. *Citrus mitis* (calamondin orange) (*see* p. 146)
* *Cycas revoluta* (Japanese sago palm) (*see* p. 103)
* *Ficus benjamina* (Java, weeping, fig) (*see* p. 104)
* *Ficus religiosa* (peepul) (*see* p. 109)
* *Gardenia jasminoides,* syn. G. augusta (Cape jasmine or common gardenia) (*see* p. 113)
* *Hibiscus rosa-sinensis* (rose of China or Chinese hibiscus) (*see* p. 146)
* *Jacaranda mimosifolia* (jacaranda) (*see* p. 147)
* *Lagerstroemia indica* (crape or crepe myrtle) (*see* p. 118)
* *Leptospermum scoparium* (manuka or New Zealand tea tree) (*see* p. 120)
* *Myrtus communis* (common myrtle) (*see* p. 126)
* *Nandina domestica* (sacred bamboo or heavenly bamboo) (*see* p. 127)
* *Olea europaea* (common olive) (*see* p. 128)
* *Pistacia lentiscus* (mastic tree or lentisc) (*see* p. 131)
* *Punica granatum* var. *nana* (dwarf pomegranate) (*see* p. 135)
* *Styrax japonicus* (Japanese snowball) (*see* p. 141)
* *Ulmus parviflora* (Chinese or lacebark elm) (*see* p. 142)

Seeds of Camellia japonica *(common camellia) should only be sown in spring or early summer, in an acidic potting mix, using pots or seed trays.*

Sowing seeds in a greenhouse

The best place in which to sow and germinate seeds is in a heated greenhouse or sunroom. Shaded windowsills can be used, but usually the temperature varies widely and may cause the potting mix to be either too hot or too cold. Also, because of this temperature change, moisture in the potting mix fluctuates and, if it becomes too dry, young seedlings die. Conversely, potting mix that is too wet encourages the presence of diseases, causing the seedlings to collapse.

Seeds need warmth, moisture and air to initiate germination; most also need darkness. Those seeds that do not require darkness to encourage germination are very small and often dustlike. Here is the way to sow seeds:

1

Fill a plastic seed tray with seed-starting mix. Firm it with your fingers, especially around the edges, as this is where loose mix first starts to become dry if watering is neglected. Always check that the drainage holes in the base of a seed tray are not blocked.

2

Refill the seed tray with more seed-starting mix and use a straight-edged piece of wood to level the mix to the rim of the container. Then use a flat piece of thick wood (slightly smaller in area than the inside of the seed tray and with a small block of wood attached to the top to provide a handle) to evenly press down the mix's surface to about ½ inch (12 mm) below the rim. Adding a layer of sharp sand encourages germination when sowing seeds of outdoor bonsai in seed trays.

③ Fold a piece of stiff paper — preferably a light color so that seeds placed on it can be easily seen — and tip a few seeds onto it. Then, gently tap the end of the folded paper to encourage the seeds to fall evenly over the potting mix. Do not sow seeds within ½ inch (12 mm) of the sides of the seed tray, as this is where the potting mix first becomes dry if watering is neglected. Always ensure that the seeds are evenly spaced. Use the pointed blade of a knife or a pair of tweezers to move them if they fall in clusters.

④ Use a flat-bottomed horticultural sieve to cover the seeds with potting mix to three or four times their thickness. A few seeds need light to encourage germination, while others need only a very thin covering. If a horticultural sieve is not available, use an old kitchen sieve. Ensure that the seeds are evenly covered. Only small and dustlike seeds do not need to be covered.

⑤ Carefully stand the seed tray in a flat-bottomed plastic bowl filled shallowly with water. When moisture seeps to the surface of the potting mix, remove the seed tray and allow the water to drain. Do not water from overhead, as this washes the seeds into clusters. Label the seed tray with the name of the seeds, as well as the date of sowing.

⑥ Stand the seed tray in a greenhouse and cover it with a sheet of clear glass. Condensation that accumulates on the underside must be wiped off every day and the glass then turned over. Alternatively, cover the seed tray with a plastic dome. An even temperature is needed, of about 64–72°F (18–22°C).

⑦ To create a dark environment, cover the glass or plastic dome with a few sheets of newspaper. As soon as the seeds germinate, remove the paper and lower the temperature. Excessive warmth encourages seedlings to grow too fast and to become thin and weak.

❗ The four elements

Moisture is essential to soften the outer coat of the seed and activate chemical processes that initiate the growth of roots and leaves.

Warmth quickens the growth processes. Plants from temperate regions need less warmth than those native to the tropics. High temperatures tend to encourage rapid germination, which often results in weak seedlings.

Air causes chemical changes within the seed, and is essential for normal growth processes and respiration. Well-aerated potting mix is important.

Darkness and light are important for germination. Most seeds germinate in darkness, although a few germinate better in light. After germination, light is essential to activate the plant's growth processes. Photosynthesis can only take place in sunlight.

Transplanting seedlings

Take care when handling seedlings, as their stems are easily bruised and damaged. Always hold seedlings by one of their seed leaves, rather than attempt to grip a stem. Most seedlings have two seed leaves, a few have just one. Follow this sequence to transfer seedlings and to space them more widely apart:

①

After germination, remove the covering and continue to water the seedlings by standing the seed tray in a bowl shallowly filled with water. When moisture seeps to the surface of the potting mix, remove the tray and allow excess moisture to drain. Avoid wetting the leaves as this encourages the onset of disease, especially if the temperature is low. A damp environment and low temperatures trigger fungal diseases such as *Pythium debaryanum* and *Phytophthora cryptogea*.

②

When the leaves of seedlings touch each other, transfer them to another seed tray where they can be spaced more widely apart. The day before transplanting, water the potting mix. Use a spoon or fork to carefully lift a cluster of seedlings from the seed tray and place them on a damp piece of hessian (sack cloth) or newspaper. Ensure that their roots do not dry out.

It is better to transplant young and small seedlings than to leave them until they are tall and crowded. Young seedlings become established more readily than older ones with stems that have already become slightly hardened. Never squeeze the soft stems when transplanting.

3

Fill another seed tray with potting mix and firm it to ½ inch (12 mm) below the rim. Use a small dibber to make holes about ¾ inch (18 mm) deep, keeping the outer rows ½–¾ inch (12–18 mm) from the sides. Plant the seedlings individually. Hold each seedling by a leaf, not its stem, and position it so that its roots dangle freely into a hole. Use the dibber (or a chopstick for very small seedlings) to level potting mix around the roots.

4

When the seed tray is full, gently tap its edges to level the loose potting mix. Then, stand it on a level, free-draining surface and water gently using a watering can with an oval, upward-facing rose. When using a spray-type watering device, ensure that the seedlings are not unnecessarily disturbed. This helps to settle potting mix around the roots. Do not place young seedlings in strong sunlight as it is difficult for them to take in moisture until their roots are established.

Potting up young plants

After weeks — or months, depending on the species — the seed tray will become crowded as the young plants' foliage develops. At this stage, they should be transferred into individual pots.

The day before you pot up your plants, water the potting mix and allow the excess moisture to drain. Fill the bases of a few small pots with potting mix so that when the plants are potted the old soil marks on the stems are fractionally below the surface of the potting mix, which should be about ½ inch (12 mm) below the rim of the pots.

Gently hold a plant by its stem, check its depth relative to the pot and trickle potting mix around its roots, firming it gently afterward. When potting is complete, carefully water to settle the potting mix evenly around the roots. Remember to label each pot with the plant's name, as well as the date it was potted.

Above: *When young plants that initially grew relatively closely together in seed trays are transferred to small pots or bags, they soon take advantage of the additional room for their roots and extra space for their leaves and stems. During this period, keep the potting mix lightly moist, not saturated, with water.*

Raising indoor bonsai from cuttings

Many indoor bonsai can be raised from softwood and hardwood cuttings. Unless you have access to a neglected indoor bonsai, avoid using young shoots pruned from established bonsai. This is seldom practical and the best solution is to take cuttings from houseplants.

Softwood cuttings

Softwood cuttings can be taken at any time, but spring or early summer, when the mother plant is actively growing, is best. Some experts recommend cuttings up to 6 inches (15 cm) long, but those that are 2-3 inches (5-7.5 cm) in length have a better chance of forming roots. Here is a step-by-step guide to preparing and rooting softwood cuttings:

- Use a clean pot and fill it with a mixture of equal parts sharp sand and moist peat moss. Firm the surface to about ½ inch (12 mm) below the pot's rim. Additionally, sprinkle a thin layer of sharp sand over the surface.

- Use a sharp knife or pair of scissors to sever a shoot. Cut the shoot just above a leaf joint, so that a short stub of stem is not left on the mother plant. If a stub is left, it will decay, become unsightly and encourage diseases to enter the plant.

- Using the sharp knife, sever the cutting fractionally below the bottom leaf joint. Cut off the lower leaves, taking care not to damage the base of the bud (or buds) in the leaf joints. At this point, the cutting should be 2-3 inches (5-7.5 cm) long.

- To speed up the development of roots, dip the base of the cutting in a hormone rooting powder. The more quickly a cutting develops roots, the less chance the base has of decaying.

- Use a small dibber to form a 1-1½-inch (2.5-3.5 cm) deep hole. A small pot, 2½-3 inches (6.5-7.5 cm) wide, can hold one cutting, while a 5-inch (13 cm) wide pot is suitable for three to five cuttings. Do not space them closer than ¾ inch (18 mm) to the edges of the pot.

- Hold a cutting by a leaf and suspend the cutting in the hole. Ensure that the cutting is upright and use a dibber to firm the mix around the stem.

- When the pot is full, use a watering can with the rose facing upright, so that water gently sprays onto the surface of the mix, settling it around each cutting's stem.

- Place the pot in a propagating unit (where high humidity can be provided), or insert three short stakes into the mix and draw a plastic bag over them. Use an elastic band to hold the bag firmly in place around the pot's base. Regularly check that the compost is moist. When small shoots start to develop from the cutting, remove the plastic bag and reduce the temperature. Later, plants can be individually transferred into a pot and allowed to grow and become established before being trained into an indoor bonsai.

! Mist propagation

Commercial nurseries use mist propagation units to encourage softwood cuttings to develop roots. The equipment is electrically operated and is designed to maintain a thin film of water droplets over the cuttings. This keeps them cool, and prevents the leaves from wilting until the bases of their stems develop roots and can be transferred to individual pots.

Small mist-propagation units are available for home use. In addition to the mist of water, they provide warmth for the bases of the cuttings to accelerate rooting.

Cuttings are usually prepared and inserted into pots holding equal parts of moist peat and sharp sand, and placed on the base of the propagation unit. Alternatively — and especially for large numbers of cuttings — a 3-4 inch (7.5-10 cm) thick bed of moist peat and sharp sand is spread over the warming cables, and cuttings are inserted directly into it. Do not provide too much heat — adhere to the manufacturer's instructions — and transfer the cuttings to pots as soon as roots form.

Half-ripe cuttings

Also known as semi-mature, semi-ripe and semi-hardwood cuttings, these are shoots that are more mature than softwood types (*see* p. 25) yet not as mature as hardwood cuttings (*see* p. 27). It is a vegetative method of increasing deciduous and evergreen shrubs, as well as heathers and many conifers. Normally, cuttings are 4–5 inches (10–13 cm) long and best taken from non-bonsai subjects. Taking half-ripe cuttings from indoor bonsai soon spoils their shape. It is better to take them from houseplants, perhaps when converting them into bonsai.

Half-ripe cuttings are normally taken during midsummer and into the early part of late summer. Some cuttings are taken with a heel (a small piece of bark or wood left at the base of a cutting), while others are just severed beneath a leaf joint.

Here is a step-by-step guide to taking half-ripe cuttings:

- Select a healthy half-ripe shoot, 4–5 inches (10–13 cm) long. When taking a heel cutting, carefully pull off the shoot from its branch, remove the lower leaves and trim the whiskerlike theads from around the heel. Heels encourage rapid rooting, as well as give the cuttings greater stability when inserted into the potting mix. On cuttings without heels, remove their lower leaves and cut their bases just below a leaf joint.

- Dip the base of each cutting in hormone rooting powder and insert into 1½–2 inches (3.5–5 cm) equal parts moist peat and sharp sand in a pot 3–5 inches (7.5–13 cm) wide. Three cuttings usually fit into a 3-inch (7.5 cm) wide pot, whereas five can fit in a 5-inch (13 cm) one. Do not position the cuttings close to the pot's edge. Firm the potting mix around the base of each cutting, then water from above to thoroughly moisten the mix.

- Place the pot of cuttings on a bed of coarse sand in the base of a cold frame (*see* opposite). Shade from strong sunlight and ventilate during hot periods. During summer, lightly mist the plants with water to keep the potting mix moist and to cool the foliage. This reduces a cutting's need to absorb moisture from the potting mix before roots are formed. Some cuttings, especially from specific tropical and subtropical plants, also need warmth.

- In warm climates it is possible to place the pots of cuttings outside in a shaded position, but ensure that the potting mix and cuttings do not become excessively hot.

- Rooting is not rapid and often it is not until the following spring that the cuttings have roots.

1

1. **Half-ripe cuttings with heels**: Using a healthy shoot, carefully pull it away from its parent shoot. Cut off the lower leaves and trim off whiskerlike threads from the heel (at the base of the cutting).

2. **Half-ripe cuttings without heels**: Insert several cuttings in a clean pot filled with equal parts moist peat and sharp sand that is evenly firmed. Firm potting mix around each cutting's base and water it gently.

2

These are chemicals that have been used for many years to encourage the development of roots on cuttings, especially softwood types that need to produce roots before their bases start to decay. Most hormone rooting powders include fungicides to help prevent diseases from entering the cut end.

Rather than dipping the end of a cutting into the actual container of rooting powder, it is better to tip a small amount into a lid (other than that of the hormone powder) and to dip each cutting's base into it. This prevents the powder from being ruined if the cutting is exceptionally moist and water drips onto the powder. However, should the cutting's base have become dry and not retain any of the powder, first dip it in water, then shake off the excess moisture before inserting it into the powder.

Always store the powder in a dry place. In damp situations, put the container holding the powder into another container, such as a large screw-top jar. Ensure that the container and jar are clearly labeled.

Hardwood cuttings

These are formed from mature shoots of the current season's growth, mainly from early to late autumn, although cuttings can be taken up to early spring. They are much larger than half-ripe cuttings and range from 6–15 inches (15–38 cm) in length.

Indoor bonsai are tropical and subtropical plants that mostly have an evergreen nature, and therefore are not usually increased by hardwood cuttings. However, many traditional bonsai, which are hardy outdoor plants, can be increased in this way.

Using a cold frame

If half-ripe cuttings are exposed to high temperatures and the same conditions as softwood cuttings, they will die before they can produce roots. For this reason, cold frames are recommended because they protect small plants from excessive cold and wet weather. Cold frames are easily constructed. They consist of a wood or brick surround, covered with glass secured within a wooden framework.

Below: *Traditionally, a cold frame is unheated and the sides are 9–12 inches (23–30 cm) high — sometimes slightly higher for tall plants. Position the cold frame in a wind-sheltered area, with the glass sloping toward the main source of sunlight.*

Converting a young houseplant to a bonsai

Converting a houseplant is an inexpensive, easy and relatively quick way to create an indoor bonsai (many of the species that can be converted in this way are detailed on pp. 90–144).

In traditional Japanese bonsai the focus is on the cultivation of hardy shrubs, trees and conifers found in temperate climates —these can be gathered from the wild (with the permission of the landowner), potted and converted into a bonsai. With indoor bonsai, it is far easier and more predictable to buy and convert young, healthy houseplants from a garden center. In temperate climates these include many tropical and subtropical plants, such as the *Ficus* species and many small-leaved types of plants. Other houseplants that can be converted include the *Bougainvillea* x *buttiana* 'Mrs. Butt,' with its distinctively purplish-red bracts (modified leaves), *Crassula ovata* (jade plant), *Jacaranda mimosifolia* (jacaranda), *Hibiscus rosa-sinensis* (rose of China) and *Schefflera actinophylla* (Australian ivy palm).

A few considerations

When buying a small young houseplant for the purpose of converting it into an indoor bonsai, check that it is healthy and free from pests and diseases. Houseplants need to be converted in a systematic way. Here are a few basic considerations:

- Before buying a plant, visualize the style you wish to achieve and try to picture the plant when pruned and shaped. This will avoid the unnecessary removal of branches and allow you to achieve the desired style quickly and easily.
- Apart from the style, bear in mind the shape and type of container. Color and shape considerations are suggested on p. 60, and these can further enhance a plant.
- When considering a flowering houseplant, do not attempt to convert it while it is flowering; not only can it be difficult to see the plant's shape, but its seasonal beauty will be lost.
- Buy a young and healthy plant, preferably in spring when it is showing signs of new growth. A thick trunk, especially at the base, will later give the bonsai an aged look, while equally spaced branches — at about right angles to the trunk — are ideal for creating the formal upright style (*see* p. 38).
- Initially, cut away unnecessary branches. Later, cut back the main branches to the desired length, always cutting to just beyond a bud to prevent shoots from dying and leaving stubs.

- After choosing a tree's design and making the initial conversion, allow the plant to settle down. About three weeks later, remove it from its pot, trim the roots and repot it into a prepared bonsai container. The way to prepare a container for potting a bonsai is described on pp. 65–66.
- It will take several months for a plant to settle into its new environment and style before new growth appears. Do not water the plant excessively during this period.
- The shape and color of the container you buy are also influenced by the decor of the room. Brightly colored containers create a dramatic contrast against white walls, while pastel-colored containers create a more relaxed look.

Opposite: *Various houseplants can be used, including* Ficus benjamina *'Starlight'* (right)*;* Crassula sarcocaulis, *with its narrow and attractively variegated leaves* (front)*; and* Buxus sempervirens *'Faulkner' (boxwood)* (back).

Four popular styles to create from houseplants

On this and the following pages, four different styles of bonsai are illustrated and the techniques of modifying them explained in detail. These styles include both formal and informal bonsai. Species pictured in this section include *Buxus sempervirens* 'Faulkner' (boxwood), *Ficus benjamina* (Java fig) and *Crassula sarcocaulis*.

Formal and upright

1. Carefully select a plant with an upright stance and an even number of branches well covered in leaves.

2. Prune off the lower branches, as well as the small and thin ones higher up, to produce an uncluttered trunk. Leave the main branches in place.

③ As more branches and shoots are removed, its shape becomes distinctive. Pliable shoots can be given a lower lateral position by gently pressing them at their junction with the trunk.

④ About three weeks after the major pruning, transfer the plant to a bonsai container. This repotting involves cutting back the roots.

1

2

Choose a plant that has a pliable trunk with a natural bend one-third of the way up from its base. The plant need not have an even number of branches on the trunk, and they don't need to be of equal thickness. There should, however, be many of them to allow for a greater choice of which ones to cut off when creating the desired shape.

Cut off a few low and thin shoots to create a bare base for the trunk. Select the face side (front) of the plant and insert a stout bamboo cane into the potting mix, midway between the side of the pot and trunk. Carefully manipulate the lower part of the trunk into a sideways U-shape; secure the trunk to the cane. Then bend the upper part of the trunk, so that it re-crosses the cane; again, secure the trunk to the cane.

③

④

At this stage, cut off small and thin shoots from the rest of the trunk to create an easily recognizable shape with a trunk that has a large curve toward its base and a small one above it. The branches on each side of the trunk should add to the design and, although different, they must be in visual balance with each other.

Slowly the trunk will assume the desired shape, until the time arrives when the cane and ties can be removed. At this stage, the trunk may lose its well-defined bends, but only slightly. Adding wires (see pp. 46–49 for details on wiring) helps the plant retain its shape. About three or four weeks later, transfer the plant to a new pot.

For this style to be successful, select a houseplant with a strong, well-defined main trunk, and another one growing from its base. They should not be the same size or thickness, as this visually confuses the eye and detracts from the concept of the style. Check that the plant is well clothed in branches and leaves, especially in its upper parts, which will give you a bigger choice later when you must decide what to cut off.

Use sharp pruning shears to cut off branches from the bottom of the main trunk. Prune the smaller trunk similarly. If you are in doubt about a branch, leave it in place until later when it can be quickly and easily pruned to complement the shape.

To enable the two trunks to be readily seen, cut off branches that grow toward each other. At the same time, reduce the number of branches so that the bonsai has an uncluttered look.

Allow the plant to settle down and for shoots to appear before transferring it to a bonsai container. The base of the trunk can be positioned slightly above the rim of the container as this helps to accentuate the style. This will make more frequent watering essential, however. Immersing the pot is an effective method of watering.

Multitrunk

① Selecting a suitable plant is fundamental to this style. A single-root system and several different-sized trunks are essential. Initially the plant may appear congested, but try to visualize it once pruning is complete.

② Keep the plant in the pot in which it was bought to provide a firm base. Start modifying the plant by cutting off one-third of the branches from the lower part of each trunk. As you continue to prune and remove crossing branches, each trunk will become better defined. Shaping the bonsai's outline is also important.

③ After three or four weeks, transfer the plant to its bonsai container. A round or rectangular container suits this style.

Chapter 2

Choosing and training indoor bonsai

I n temperate and colder climates, tropical or subtropical plants must be grown indoors. They are encouraged to remain small by restricting the root system as well as by regular pruning. In this chapter, specific information is provided on training indoor bonsai whether established, bought from a nursery or garden center, or raised by seed or from a cutting. Suggested styles and shapes are explored and indicated for specific species, and various pruning and wiring techniques are explained – in particular root, branch, shoot and leaf pruning, as well as shaping a trunk or branch.

Opposite: *Wiring encourages bonsai to adopt and maintain an attractive shape.*

Styles of bonsai

Indoor bonsai can be grown in many shapes and styles, and featured here is a wide range to consider. Furthermore, check the type, shape and color of the container as these have a dramatic influence on the display (*see* pp. 57–60 for details).

The shape and style of indoor bonsai mirror that of traditional bonsai, which have evolved over many years. They range from upright to cascade and can simulate slanting or windswept looks. Their outlines are miniature impressions of plants growing in the wild that have been shaped by their environment. For example, a wild plant that is exposed to continual and strong wind usually has branches on one side only — a feature replicated by the "windswept" style. Similarly, a group of trees on a slight hill is reflected in the "group" style (*see* p. 41), and a plant growing at the edge of a cliff with branches that lean and cascade is depicted by the "cascade" look.

Some styles — such as informal upright, formal upright and cascade — are especially popular as they can be applied to many plants. Others are not so widely attempted but are highly attractive nevertheless.

The most important identification of a style is the angle at which the trunk grows in the container. For example, a formal and upright tree is, by nature and definition, upright and with branches that create an approximately triangular outline, whereas an informal and upright tree has a leaning or bent trunk that reveals a more relaxed nature.

Some styles suit one species, but not others. In "The A to Z of Bonsai" (pp. 88–147), a range of styles are recommended to suit each of the described plants. (The details of achieving these styles, through wiring and pruning, are to be found on pp. 42–49.)

At the same time as deciding on a particular style, select a position where your bonsai can be displayed. Essential to cascading types, for example, is a display stand or shelf from where branches can hang freely.

 ## Formal upright

Sometimes known as formal and upright, this style features an upright trunk and branches that create a triangular outline. Although formal, the shape is not strictly symmetrical. The branches are usually horizontal or slightly drooping, their thickness decreasing from the lower ones to those at the top.

This style especially suits needle-bearing conifers, but not fruit trees or ones with a definite informal growth pattern (that is, one that is curved and angular).

Informal upright

Sometimes also known as informal and upright, this style has a similar nature to the formal upright form, but has an irregular triangular outline and an informally curved trunk. The trunk leans not more than 15 degrees from either right to left or left to right, but not toward the viewer.

Both evergreen and deciduous trees suit this relaxed, informal style, which often attracts more attention than the formal upright type.

Leaning

In this style, sometimes known as slanting style, the trunk leans throughout most of its length, at an angle of about 45 degrees. Branches grow from both sides of the trunk (unlike the windswept style), horizontally or with a slight droop. Usually, but not essentially, they grow alternately from the trunk, rather than opposite each other.

The leaning style suits many deciduous and evergreen plants. However, it is especially attractive for evergreen conifers.

Cascade

This relaxed and informal style replicates the shape of a tree growing at the edge of a cliff and cascading into space. The tip of the cascading branch extends beyond the base of the container to create an especially attractive feature. Because of the length of the main stem, it is essential to display the bonsai on a high, decorative stand.

This style suits evergreen and deciduous plants, as well as conifers and flowering bonsai.

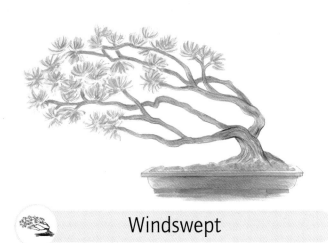

Windswept

This bonsai has the appearance of growing on a windswept moor, coast or cliff top. Unlike leaning bonsai, it only has branches on one side. The angle of the trunk and branches is more acute than that of the leaning style, with relatively few branches.

Conifers are especially suited to the windswept style, which is very distinctive. It should not compete with other bonsai when it is displayed as a room feature.

Semi-cascade

This is similar in concept to the cascade style, but it is not so pendulous. Initially, the main branch grows at an angle slightly above the horizontal, then cascades (but not radically) with its tip at a level halfway between the top and bottom of the container.

The semi-cascade style suits many bonsai, but not those with a strongly upright nature. Many evergreen and deciduous trees are suitable; flowering trees are also attractive when presented in this style.

Types of pruning

Here are three main approaches to creating a bonsai by pruning:

- Buying an established bonsai and performing maintenance pruning. The techniques and timing for this depend on whether the bonsai is evergreen or deciduous.
- Buying a small houseplant and converting it to a bonsai. This is often known as "subtractive pruning" or "pruning to shape," and it involves buying a young plant and converting it, through radical pruning, to assume an attractive shape (*see* pp. 28–35 for details). Later, maintenance pruning is needed.
- Starting with small, young plants, perhaps seed raised or from cuttings, and undertaking regular pruning over several years to create a bonsai. This is known as the "addition method."

Root pruning

Root pruning is an integral part of repotting an established bonsai, and involves cutting off about a third of the roots and repotting the root ball into a clean container (*see* p. 68). Additionally, root pruning is undertaken when repotting a young houseplant to convert it into an indoor bonsai.

When a bonsai is root pruned, more space is made available for the potting mix. Outdoor bonsai are best root pruned in spring, but indoor types can be repotted and root pruned anytime, although spring or early summer is still best.

Branch pruning

Branch pruning is the main influence on the shape and size of an indoor bonsai and can be performed at any time when the plant is growing strongly, but preferably in spring and early summer. There are several general pruning techniques to consider:

- The position of a cut influences the direction of the shoot that develops from the bud (immediately below the cut). Always check if the bud will produce a shoot in the desired direction.
- Allow the shoots of a young plant to grow longer than those of an older plant before pruning. This encourages the development of strong, firm shoots.
- Prune older bonsai more frequently and earlier than you would young plants.
- Occasionally, when a tree is congested with branches, it may be necessary to remove a complete branch. In this case, cut the branch back in several pieces before using concave branch cutters (*see* p. 54) to cut the remaining piece close to the trunk.

Pruning

Pruning is an essential part of creating and looking after an indoor bonsai. Roots, branches, shoots and leaves are the parts of a bonsai that are pruned. The main purpose of pruning, apart from maintaining general health, is to create a small and desirable shape.

Pruning roots initially appears to be a drastic way to enable plants to be grown in small containers, but additional roots soon grow at an alarming rate to stabilize the plant and absorb plant foods from the soil. Root pruning is performed whenever a plant is repotted.

Above: *Always use strong, sharp pruning tools when root pruning; inferior blades will buckle.*
Opposite: *Use strong branch cutters to sever a branch close to the trunk without damaging its bark.*

This prevents damaging the remaining branches should the cutting tool slip while in use.

- When pruning a branch, ensure the cut is clean, as clean cuts heal more rapidly than a cut with a jagged edge.
- When initially pruning a young plant, cut out branches growing from the lower third of the trunk.
- Ensure the branches project to the sides, not forward. Some can project back, but they must not create excessive visual or physical weight that could result in an imbalance.
- Avoid having two branches arising on opposite sides of the trunk and at about the same position. It is better to have an alternating sequence of branches up the trunk. They should also be spaced apart and not cause congestion.
- Cut out crossing branches and those that disturb the harmony. If left, they congest the central part of the arrangement and reduce air circulation.

Shoot pruning

Shoots are soft and relatively new growth. If left, they develop into branches that clothe the bonsai, but if pruning is neglected they can soon swamp the plant with leaves and stems, causing it to lose shape and become unsightly. Here are a few clues to successful shoot pruning:

❧ Shoot pruning can be undertaken throughout the year on tropical and many subtropical plants, but it is essential that the plant be growing strongly.
For that reason, pruning during spring and summer is ideal.

❧ Do not prune if the plant is in flower.

❧ Always use sharp scissors and cut just above a bud without damaging it.

❧ Cut back a shoot to just above a bud to encourage growth in the desired direction. For instance, cut a lateral shoot to just beyond a downward-facing bud if the required direction is horizontal. Cutting a shoot to just beyond an upward-facing bud encourages upright growth.

❧ Shoots are best trimmed when they start to thicken. Pruning shoots that have six to eight pairs of leaves is ideal; cut back to two or three pairs of leaves.

2. Always use sharp scissors. There is a wide range available; those with long handles and pointed blades are ideal for severing shoots in difficult positions. Discard all severed shoots.

3. Always cut a shoot to just above a leaf joint, taking care not to leave short spurs, which eventually die back. As well as being unsightly, they encourage the presence of diseases. Preferably, make an angled cut, but do not damage the bud or leave it protruding above the severed shoot.

1. After shoots are pruned, more shoots develop from leaf joints below the cut. Shoots that are pruned well back eventually produce stronger shoots than those that are only lightly pruned. More bonsai are spoiled by being too lightly pruned than by being trimmed slightly more severely.

Leaf pruning

Leaf pruning needs a more delicate touch than branch pruning, and sharp scissors are essential. Here are a few clues to successful leaf pruning:

- Plants native to tropical and subtropical regions can be leaf pruned at any time, but preferably in spring as soon as growth resumes.
- If the plant is not growing strongly and its health is suspect, spread leaf pruning over two weeks. This will reduce the risk of shock. Prune the largest leaves first and the smaller ones later.
- Prune each leaf separately, cutting back nearly to the base of the leaf stalk, but taking care not to damage the dormant bud at the axil. Preferably, leave a short stub known as a sprout axil.
- You may feel the need to remove all the leaves of your bonsai to encourage a fresh crop of smaller, more dainty leaves, but do not do so more than once a season and not after summer repotting. Initially, this creates an unattractive plant, but fresh new leaves will appear in six to eight weeks.
- Do not water the plant excessively after pruning, especially if all the leaves were removed, as it will not be as active as it previously was. Slowly increase the amount of water as the leaves reappear.

Flowering trees

Flowering trees are seldom leaf pruned, especially if their leaves are small. If leaf pruning does become necessary, tackle it after the flowers have faded and remove only the large leaves.

Right: *Leaf pruning needs more care and thought than root or shoot pruning. Water one day before pruning, as leaves and shoots are easier to cut when they are full of moisture.*

Wiring an indoor bonsai

When training a bonsai to assume a desired shape, pruning is sometimes not enough and wiring becomes necessary. This involves winding wires around the trunk or branches and leaving them in position until the desired shape has been achieved. Several types of wire can be used:

- Annealed-copper and anodized-aluminum wires (*see* glossary, p. 149) are popular. (Annealing is when wire is heated up until it glows red and then is allowed to cool slowly. This softens it and makes it easier to manipulate. Anodization entails coating the metal with a protective film by chemical or electrolytic processes.)
- Copper wire, in general, is least obtrusive; anodized or colored aluminum is similarly inconspicuous.
- Annealed-copper wire is recommended for use on conifers as it best supports soft textured bark. The copper wire is wound onto the branches and then hardens as it is worked, providing the necessary support to position the branches into precise designs. However, with age it tends to harden and may damage the bark when it is removed.
- Soft aluminum wire is ideal for deciduous trees as it does not damage the bark.
- In principle, both copper and the lighter colored and softer aluminum wires can be reused, though copper wire needs to be reannealed before it can be used for a second time. However, since wires are often removed in pieces, reuse is seldom possible.

- Wires are available in several thicknesses to suit various tasks and are graded in gauges. Those between 12 and 20 are most commonly used. The higher the number the thinner the wire. As a guide, choose a gauge that is one-sixth to one-third the diameter of the branch or trunk being shaped. If the branch or trunk is not pliable, use a wire that is one-third its thickness.

When to wire an indoor bonsai

It is best to wire indoor bonsai when they are growing strongly and their sap is flowing freely. That invariably means during summer. Soft, sappy bark is easily damaged, so wire with care.

Most indoor bonsai are evergreen. Some lose their leaves in cold or temperate conditions. Although it is easier to wire leafless plants, wait until growth resumes in spring or early summer.

Below: *The range of wires used to shape trunks and branches is wide. Take care when handling wire not to create kinks and to store it in coils. Before use, ensure wires are at room temperature and malleable; wires stored in a cold shed can be difficult to use.*

How long should the wires remain in position?

After wiring a bonsai, regularly check that the wires are not cutting into the bark. The time it takes until a trunk or branch will remain in the desired shape depends on the plant, its age and shape. Young branches will assume and retain a shape quicker than old ones, and thick branches take longer than thin ones.

As an approximation, evergreen subjects take up to nine months (sometimes more) to accept a new form; deciduous ones are quicker to shape. Three to six months often brings good results. Indoor bonsai accept and maintain a new shape quicker than traditional outdoor types.

Remove wires with care. It is often easier to remove them in small pieces, rather than as a complete length. If the branch is damaged, paint with a wound sealant. Avoid nipping the bark with pointed cutters when removing wires.

Getting the wiring technique right

The angle at which wire is wound around a trunk or branch influences its ability to hold it in place. A 45-degree angle provides the greatest strength for a given thickness of wire. Closer coils act like a spring and power is compromised. In the instances where this occurs, use thicker wire instead.

For uniformity and ease of application, wind the wire in a counterclockwise direction and at the correct angle. An angle wider than 45 degrees results in wires that are too far apart. Unevenly wound wires are ineffective and unsightly. Wire needs to be wound close to the bark; if too loose it will not hold the branch in position, but if too tight it will cut into the bark. Before wiring a bonsai – whether a trunk or branch – practice on a houseplant or even a pruned and discarded branch.

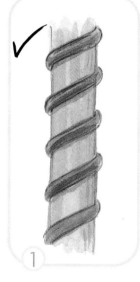

1
The wire is wound evenly and is sufficiently tight to hold the branch or trunk in place, but not so tight that it can damage the bark.

2
Wire loops are spaced too far apart and will not hold the branch or trunk in the desired position.

3
Unevenly spaced and unsightly. Wire is ineffective in holding a branch or trunk in place.

4
The wire is too loose and will not hold a trunk or branch in the desired position.

5
The wire is too tight. It is cutting into the bark and will damage the plant.

Shaping a trunk

Cut a length of wire slightly more than one-third longer than the length of the trunk of your bonsai and of a suitable thickness (*see* p. 46). Wire it in a systematic way (*see* figures 1–3).

Note that:

∞ Sometimes it is necessary to double-wire a trunk (occasionally, thick branches as well). Only those trunks that are thick and cannot be easily shaped by a single piece of wire need to be double wired. This involves adding a second wire. After the first wire is in place, insert the end of another one into the soil at the base of the plant and wind it just below the first one. Do not cross the first wire.

∞ Only once the wire (or wires) is in place, can you slowly manipulate the trunk into the desired position.

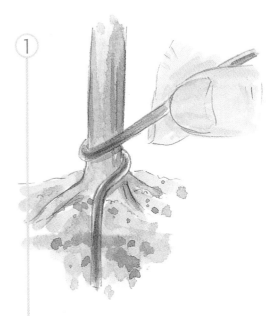

1. Insert one end of the wire vertically or at a slight angle into the soil, on the side of the plant that is least attractive and is away from the main viewing position. This will hold the end secure. Then, in a counterclockwise direction — and, initially, almost horizontally — wind the wire up the trunk at a 45-degree angle.

2 and 3. Continue to wire the rest of the trunk without deviating onto a branch.

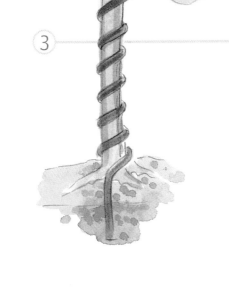

Shaping a branch

Thinner wire is usually needed for branches. Start wiring from the lowest branch and work upward. When the wires are in position, gently manipulate the branch (or branches) into the desired shape.

❦ Choose a piece of wire of the right thickness (*see* p. 46); cut it about one-third longer than the length of the branch to be shaped.

❦ Take care when manipulating branches into a desired shape not to strain and damage them. Old branches are more likely to be damaged than younger pliable ones.

1. Lie the end of the length of wire against the branch as shown. When the wire reaches the trunk, wrap it once around the trunk in a clockwise direction and then under and over around the branch you wish to wire.

2. For two branches growing approximately opposite each other, one piece of wire can be used. The wire is first looped over the branch, not from underneath, which may result in the branch snapping when bent.

3. When you need to shape two branches that are spaced wide apart, you can also wrap the wire around the trunk.

Chapter 3

Looking after
your bonsai

L ooking after and training an indoor bonsai is challenging as each year one needs to apply further techniques and refinements. You can buy established indoor bonsai in interesting styles from specialist nurseries and garden centers, or convert young and healthy houseplants.

Mastering all of the skills you need to look after your indoor bonsai requires several years, but early results can often be spurred on by visiting specialist bonsai nurseries and looking at the many ways plants have been trained. Exhibitions of indoor bonsai also provide inspiration, as do bonsai clubs and associations.

This chapter lists the tools and equipment you will need, provides information on different types of potting mix, and describes how to pot, repot, water and feed your bonsai.

Opposite: *Ensure you have all the necessary tools and materials present prior to pruning, wiring or feeding a bonsai. This is important when repotting, as roots should not be allowed to become dry while you search for suitable tools and potting mix. Pictured here is a* Pyracantha *species (firethorn).*

Pruning tools and equipment

Your pruning tools need to be matched to the size and type of bonsai. Large plants with thick branches require strong tools; small and young plants need more delicate pieces of equipment. Never strain a small cutting tool on a thick or tough branch.

Saws are essential for thick branches, and the fine-toothed types produce a clean cut. A sharp knife is useful, as are sharp parrot-type (also known as crossover or bypass) pruning shears. Anvil-type pruning shears, with sharp blades that cut against a firm metal surface, are not suitable, as they may bruise the bark.

Wound sealants are essential for covering large cuts; they aid healing and help to prevent diseases. The sealant is easily applied by squeezing the end of the tube, or with the aid of a spatula in the case of awkwardly positioned wounds.

Branch glue is used to hold roots in place while creating a root-on-rock style.

A turntable is a useful accessory as it allows you to work on a tree without having to move around it.

Potting tools and equipment

Potting tools are all the things you'll need for the initial potting, and later repotting, of your bonsai. Included are soil firmers, soil scoops, root hooks and potting trowels, as well as plastic mesh and sieves.

Right:

1. Scoop for adding soil to pots when potting and repotting.
2. Pieces of plastic mesh for placing in the base of a bonsai container.
3. Small potting trowel for firming soil.
4. Root hook for drawing soil from root balls when repotting.
5. Soft brush, invaluable for cleaning up plants and potting mix.
6. Root rake for drawing old potting mix away from root balls when repotting.
7. Dibbers and chopsticks are ideal for manipulating soil around roots.

Opposite:

1. Large concave branch cutter.
2. Small spherical knob cutter.
3. Small concave branch cutter.
4. Fine-toothed saw.
5. Parrot-type pruning shears
6. Folding saw.
7. Wound sealant for coating large cuts.
8. Turntable so that plants can be rotated while being worked upon.

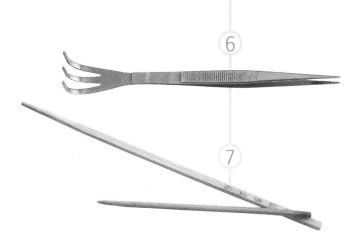

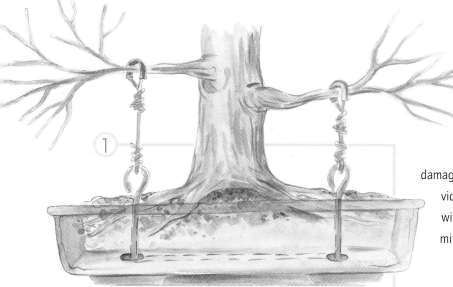

Looking after bonsai tools

Bonsai tools are expensive and after each use they should be wiped clean, allowed to dry and then rubbed with an oil-soaked cloth. Tools are best stored in a closed toolbox and put in a damp-proof shed. Dampness and rust cause the worst damage to bonsai tools. To protect them, wrap them individually in a soft cloth. Tools that become encrusted with grime will not work properly and may even transmit diseases to the plants on which they are used.

Specialist shaping tools

As you gain experience you may want to shape trunks and branches with shaping tools. Though they look like medieval torture instruments, they cause the plant no discomfort.

Homemade devices include weights that suspend about two-thirds of the way along a branch and connect to a strong piece of wood in order to uniformly straighten a leaning (slanting) trunk.

More involved items of equipment are eye-headed pieces of metal, pushed and secured through drainage holes, used to draw down branches (*see* above).

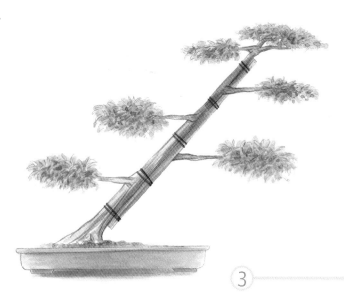

1. Levers and screws are used to draw down a branch and secure it in that position.
2. The bending jack is used to bend trunks into the desired shape.
3. A bamboo cane can keep a trunk straight and growing at a uniform angle.

Choosing containers

Garden centers and specialist bonsai nurseries stock a range of containers in many styles, shapes and colors. Before you make a choice, consider price and long-term value, as well as the fact that some bonsai styles require specific containers.

The range of styles for containers is wide and several of them are illustrated here. Always select a container with reference to a plant's style (*see* p. 60).

1. Drum type (unglazed).
2. Rectangular (glazed).
3. Semi-cascade pot (glazed).
4. Oval (glazed).
5. Rectangular (unglazed).
6. Cascade pot (unglazed).

Practical considerations

Apart from shape and style, there are a few other considerations when choosing a container:

🕸 Each container should have sufficient drainage holes in its base to enable excess water to drain freely. These holes have a further function: when pieces of wire are threaded through them they allow you to secure a plant in its growing position. Without these securing wires, most plants, especially when newly potted or repotted, would rock or topple over completely .

🕸 Small pots sometimes have only one drainage hole; wire passed through the hole would have to be looped around a non-ferrous, headless nail and slotted back through the same hole.

🕸 The container must be able to hold sufficient potting mix for the development and growth of roots.

🕸 Containers for outdoor bonsai must be frost proof. For indoor bonsai this is not a consideration, but if your bonsai collection includes outdoor and indoor plants, it is better to buy containers that are resistant to frost.

Only the outsides of bonsai containers are glazed. Glazed types are better able to withstand wet and cold conditions when left outside and acquire an attractive patina that softens their color. Many bonsai enthusiasts consider this aging an enhancement of the container, while others prefer their indoor bonsai to have a more clinical appearance, not one that reflects life outdoors.

Opposite: *Specialist nurseries and garden centers carefully store bonsai containers to protect them from breakage. Always inspect the edges of a container before buying it.*
Below: *Small containers have just one drainage hole, while larger ones have two or more.*

Range of materials used for containers

There are several materials and features that can add to the price of a container and influence your decision to buy:

- Ornate features such as fancy legs and top and bottom rims increase cost. Still, embellishments create the individuality many bonsai enthusiasts seek.
- In general, glazed containers are more expensive than unglazed ones.
- Containers that are created in a mold into which the clay material is poured, sometimes known as "poured slip" containers, are the least expensive. Nevertheless, with care they have a long life. Thin, light containers are available in most shapes, glazed and unglazed.
- Containers produced by pressing clay material into a mold are usually known as "press-mold" containers, and are slightly more expensive (their cost depends very much on the intricacies of the design). These thick and heavy containers are available in most shapes, glazed and unglazed.

- Containers shaped on a potter's wheel are known as "thrown" containers and are invariably expensive. They can be light or heavy and come in many shapes, glazed and unglazed.
- Handmade containers are costly due to the work and attention involved. They are available in many shapes.
- Antique containers are the most expensive, but their manufacture and age can be difficult to determine. Avoid containers that are glazed on the inside.

Color, style and shape

Select a container whose color, style and shape harmonize with and complement the bonsai. A wide range of bonsai styles are described and illustrated on pp. 38–41, and here are the containers to suit them:

               ❦ Broom: Especially suits round containers, as well as oval and rectangular types.

                     ❦ Cascade: Suits deep, hexagonal and octagonal containers, as well as tall round and tall square types.

                   ❦ Formal upright: Suits rectangular, square, hexagonal, octagonal, oval and round containers.

                 ❦ Group: Suits large, flat, oval and rectangular containers.

              ❦ Informal upright: Suits rectangular, square, hexagonal, octagonal, oval and round containers.

           ❦ Leaning: Also known as slanting, it suits rectangular, square, hexagonal, octagonal and oval containers.

❦ Literati: Suits round, oval or free-form containers.

❦ Multitrunk: A form of the clump style that suits oval and rectangular containers.

❦ Raft: Suits large oval and rectangular containers.

❦ Root on rock: Suits shallow, rectangular, oval and round containers.

❦ Root over rock: Suits rectangular, oval and round containers.

❦ Semi-cascade: It suits square, deep rectangular, tall and round, tall and square, as well as deep round containers.

                   ❦ Twin trunk: This form of the clump style suits oval and rectangular containers.

                   ❦ Windswept: Suits square, hexagonal, octagonal and round containers.

Above right: *The features of the* Juniperus chinensis *(Chinese juniper) are accentuated by its round glazed container. (Artist: Isabel Hofmeyr.)*
Left: *A round container* (above) *is suited to a wide range of bonsai styles, whereas a tall and square container* (below) *is ideal for cascade styles.*

Selecting suitably colored containers

Just as garden plants can display harmony or contrast, so can indoor bonsai be color coordinated with their containers. There are many flower and foliage colors and just as many containers in different colors to complement them. Remember, color choice is subjective, and the following are just guidelines:

❦ Blue flowers: Try white, yellow or orange containers.

❦ Green leaves and flowers: Try yellow, brown or, if you prefer, white containers.

❦ Orange flowers: Try blue, green, yellow or white containers, or opt for a violet alternative.

❦ Pink flowers: Try white, yellow or blue containers.

❦ Red flowers: Try yellow, blue or white containers.

❦ White flowers: Try using violet, red, blue, green or even white containers.

❦ Yellow flowers: Try red, blue, green or white containers.

Positioning the bonsai in a container

As well as color-coordinating plants and containers, and choosing containers to suit the styles of indoor bonsai, positioning the miniature trees in the pot is important and is influenced by the shape of the container. Here are a few guidelines:

- Oval container: Position the bonsai about one-third of the way along the container, midway between the back and front. Some bonsai experts suggest that the plant should be positioned slightly toward the back of the container – and this certainly suits an informal display.
- Rectangular container: Position the bonsai about one-third of the way along the container. Some experts suggest that the plant be positioned slightly toward the back of the container, while others suggest that it be along a central line. For a formal display, use a center-line position. Informal styles, where branches lean into the container, can be positioned slightly toward the rear.
- Round container: Position the bonsai in the center.
- Square container: Position the bonsai in the center.
- Tall and round containers (suitable for cascade styles): Position the bonsai in the center.
- Tall and square containers (suitable for cascade styles): Position the bonsai in the center.

Below: *A bonsai in an oval container, such as the* Juniperus procumbens *'Nana' (dwarf juniper), pictured here, looks best when positioned about one third from an end. Some authorities prefer to set it slightly toward the back. (Artist: Tony Bent.)*

Potting mix for indoor bonsai

One of the functions of potting mix is to retain moisture for the growth of plants, yet be sufficiently well drained to prevent water-logging. It must contain air to enable roots to breathe and for beneficial soil organisms to remain active. Additionally, it must contain nutrients that are readily available to the roots of plants.

Potting mix creates a secure base for a plant, holding it in place and preventing it from rocking, especially when it is newly planted. Since most bonsai containers are shallow, wires are often used to hold the plants secure (see pp. 65–66).

The term "potting mix" used here fundamentally refers to a mixture of friable loam, sand and peat, as well as plant foods. Some bonsai books call it "soil," a rather variable and imprecise term that means a mixture of clay, silt, loam, sand and organic matter (including soil organisms, some beneficial, others not) obtained from a garden.

Many bonsai growers have their own successful recipes and some rely on local ingredients to improve the moisture retention of their potting mix. Decomposed granite is used in California. Chattachoochie (see glossary, p. 149) is widely used in Florida.

Perlite and vermiculite can be added to improve water retention. Novices are advised to gain experience with one type of mix before trying another. When you buy a plant from a specialist supplier ask about the potting mix and buy a bag for future use.

Range of mixes:

You can buy ready-made proprietary potting mixes from specialist suppliers, but buy only enough for a few months. Choose securely sealed packets, as opened bags become dry and are at risk from insects. Seal the bags after use and store them in a cool, dry pest-free shed. Here is a selection of the type of mixes available:

- North American bonsai experts often use a mixture of one part crushed lava rock, one part chattachoochie, one part Texas grit and one part pine or fir bark. For trees that grow well in acid soil add two parts peat moss. Mixtures without the peat are well drained, therefore regular feeding is essential once bonsai are established in their new containers.

- British bonsai experts recommend a mix based on partially sterilized loam (harmful organisms removed — often erroneously labeled "sterilized" loam in North America), sharp sand and peat moss. Three mixtures are suggested:

Mixture one:

Basic mixture that suits most bonsai. One part partially sterilized loam, two parts sphagnum moss and two parts granite grit.

Mixture two:

A free-draining mixture ideal for plants that live in freely draining soil in their native areas. Use one part partially sterilized loam, one part sphagnum moss and three parts granite grit.

Mixture three:

This mixture is essential for plants that dislike lime. Use one part sterilized loam, three parts sphagnum moss, and one part granite grit.

- European potting mixtures are often based on partially sterilized loam. A general mixture for indoor bonsai is three parts friable loam, five parts peat moss and three parts sharp sand. For plants that need acid soil, a mixture of one part loam, five parts peat moss and two parts sharp sand is recommended.

- Succulents, especially specimens that grow large and have heavy, moisture-retentive leaves, need a heavy mix that will keep bonsai stable in their pots. Use a well-drained loam-based mix with extra coarse sand and any other heavy aggregate.

Getting the pH right

The acidity or alkalinity of a potting mix is determined on a pH scale from 0 to 14. A pH of 7.0 is chemically neutral, but most plants grow well in a pH of 6.5, which is slightly acidic. Some plants like a more acidic mix, others like one that is slightly alkaline.

The pH of your potting mix can be measured by using soil-testing kits or a pH meter. The pH of water, as well as fertilizers, also influences the pH of a mix.

Opposite: *Garden centers stock garden and houseplant potting mixes, including those suitable for indoor bonsai. Before buying, check that the bag is sealed and has not been contaminated by pests. Also, ensure that the mix is not too wet.*

Below: *The components used in bonsai potting mixes vary between continents and each country has specific preferences. At the left is milled pine bark, on the right a sample of sphagnum moss.*

Initial potting and repotting

Initial potting is when a young plant, which has been raised from seed or cuttings, is first planted in a bonsai container, or when a small, young houseplant is transferred to a container and converted into a bonsai.

Repotting happens when an established bonsai fills its container with roots and needs to be transferred to a bigger pot. How often you repot depends on the growth of the plant and whether it is young and growing rapidly, or established and not growing so vigorously. Some species of bonsai need repotting more frequently than others; an indication is given in "The A to Z of Bonsai" (pp. 88–144). Be guided by the growth of the plant and by its root density in the container.

If a bonsai has been neglected for many years and roots are appearing between the potting mix and the side of the container, then repotting is essential. When the roots of a bonsai become congested there is no space and the potting mix can no longer retain moisture and provide the plant with water and food. Growth will be severely hampered and, eventually, the plant will suffer harm.

Part of repotting involves giving fresh potting mix to the plant, as well as trimming back roots as a means to reduce and control its growth. It also allows the bonsai to be grown in a relatively small container.

Above: *This bonsai is showing signs of neglect and is in urgent need of root pruning.*

Preparing a container

Before you pot or repot a bonsai, select and prepare the new container. Select a container that harmonizes with the tree in color and shape (*see* pp. 60–61). The length of the container should be about two-thirds the height of the tree.

① Check that there are drainage holes in the base of the container to allow excess water to drain away and provide a way to anchor the plant in the pot.

② Soak the container in clean water for a day or two to ensure that it will not absorb moisture from the potting mix.

③ Cut pieces of plastic mesh to fit over the holes so that potting mix cannot pass through. Take a piece of wire and form it into a loop. Bend the ends at right angles. Insert the ends through the mesh, place the mesh over the hole, and then bend back the ends.

④ To secure the root ball in position, insert a long piece of plastic-covered wire through one hole in the base of the container and back up through the other hole. Ensure that the wire is long enough to be tied over the root ball.

⑤ If you are using a container with one hole, push the wire through the hole, around a non-ferrous headless nail, and back through the same hole. This works best on containers with legs or raised areas on the base. Flat-bottomed containers will wobble.

⑥ The final preparation stage is to cover the base with clean grit and add a thin layer of potting mix.

! Always remember

When threading wire through holes in the base of a container take care not to get kinks in it. This weakens the wire and may later make it difficult to remove when next repotting your bonsai.

Repotting an established bonsai

For best results you should repot your bonsai every two to three years. Use a dry prepared pot.

Repotting is best done at the beginning of a plant's growth cycle (usually in spring or early summer). If the plant is flowering, delay until the flowers fade. Also, select a container that is fractionally larger than the old one and complements the plant in shape and color. Here is an example of the repotting of a *Ficus natalensis* (Natal fig).

1

Using sharp wire cutters, cut any wires that were used to secure the root ball in its old container . Young plants that are growing strongly, or neglected bonsai whose roots have begun to push out of the container, will need to be released by carefully inserting a sharp knife between the root ball and the rim of the container.

! Always remember

The day before you repot your bonsai, water it thoroughly and ensure that excess moisture can drain freely. This watering will prevent damage to the roots when you remove the old potting mix, and encourage the formation of new roots once the plant has been established in its new container. Dry roots may take several weeks to recover — even with regular watering.

②

Carefully lift the root ball from the container. Use a root teaser to scrape soil from the roots without damaging them. Expose the roots underneath as well as around the root ball, using root cutters or heavy scissors to cut them back by about one-third with clean sharp cuts.

③

Place the reduced root ball in a prepared and "wired" container, and adjust the depth of potting mix in the base so that its surface is slightly below the rim — ¼ inch (6 mm) is about right at this stage and allows for later settlement of the soil when repotting. If the soil is too high it may be difficult to water the bonsai thoroughly (once repotting is complete).

Once you are sure the bonsai is correctly positioned in the container, twist the wire to secure the root ball firmly in place.

④

⑤ Sprinkle potting mix over the roots and firm it in layers, not all at once. Use a dibber (similar to a chopstick) to do this.

⑥ When the top of the potting mix is approximately ½ inch (12 mm) below the rim add a ⅛ inch (3 mm) layer of pea shingle. This helps to keep the soil moist and cool in summer.

Thoroughly water the potting mix by standing the container on a surface that drains well. Several waterings may be necessary. Alternatively, stand the container in a bowl shallowly filled with water. When moisture seeps to the surface of the soil, remove the bowl and allow the excess water to drain. When repotting is complete, keep the plant in a cool, shady spot until the roots are able to absorb moisture.

⑦

Watering

Of all the skills needed to keep an indoor bonsai healthy, watering is the most difficult to master and the one that causes the most problems. This is because the amount of water a bonsai needs varies throughout the year and is influenced by whether a plant is growing strongly or is in a dormant or semi-dormant state.

Most indoor bonsai are tropical or subtropical and, if the temperature is warm, they retain their leaves. However, some outdoor plants lose their leaves and stop growing in winter, or when the temperature drops drastically. It is these plants, particularly hardy bonsai kept outdoors, that are especially vulnerable to excessive watering. However, if a plant is growing strongly or flowering you will damage it if you do not water it enough.

Getting the balance right requires skill, particularly as sufficient moisture is necessary for active growth. If you drain the soil well and water minimally when the plant is inactive, waterlogging will not occur.

Frequency of watering

Each bonsai is unique in the amount of water it needs, but a large amount of foliage and exposure to high temperatures may increase a plant's requirements. The same goes for plants in small or shallow containers where there is little space for potting mix, or those that have not been repotted for several years.

- The alkalinity or acidity of water is measured on a pH scale. This ranges from 0 to 14, with 7.0 being neutral. A reading above 7.0 indicates alkalinity, while one below that figure indicates varying degrees of acidity. The ideal pH for most indoor bonsai is about 6.5.
- Most indoor bonsai are watered with tap water. You can keep bottles of tap water in a warm room overnight so that the water does not chill the roots and temporarily cause them to be less active.
- If you use rainwater ensure that it is clean and uncontaminated, particularly if it is runoff from a roof.
- White stains around the stem of a bonsai and on the soil indicate exposure to hard (i.e. alkaline) water. Boil hard tap water and allow it to cool before watering, or have a water softener installed in your home.

Left: *Some indoor bonsai, like this* Acer buergerianum *(trident maple), will enjoy brief spells outside in summer and can be given a quick shower of water to remove dust and to encourage greater vitality. Arrange your bonsai on a bench under a slatted roof (see p. 76), never in the full sun. (Artist: Carl Morrow).*
Below: *White stains mean that your water is alkaline. Try boiled, cooled water to prevent this unsightly effect.*

Judging when water is needed

As a general rule, plants need to be watered whenever the surface of the soil starts to become dry. The soil should always be slightly moist but never waterlogged. If it dries out, shoots and leaves will first become limp and droop, then brittle. If this happens, the plant has been neglected severely.

Type of water

- Hard water, with its high lime content, may suit some plants, but will progressively harm those that grow well in acid soil.

Applying water

Plants can be watered in several ways and each method has its own advantages:

1. The easiest way to water a bonsai is "over the rim," which means pouring water on to the potting mix from above. (Ensure that the soil is evenly watered and take care not to disturb the surface.)

2. Stand the container in a bowl shallowly filled with water. When moisture seeps to the surface of the soil, remove the container and allow the excess water to drain. Alternatively, immerse the pot in a bowl of clean water, the level of which should be just above the surface of the potting mix. Leave the pot immersed for only a few seconds. This method ensures that all of the soil is moistened. Remove the container and allow the excess water to drain. Newly potted plants, however, should not be immersed in water above the surface of the potting mix.

3. If a bonsai has been neglected and the soil allowed to become very dry, completely immerse the container in a bowl of water until bubbles stop rising to the surface. Remove and allow the excess water to drain.

Left: *If the surface of the soil becomes compacted, loosen it slightly, but take care not to disturb the roots. Compacted surface potting mix prevents water and plant foods reaching the roots.*

Feeding

Like all potted plants, bonsai need to be fed regularly. The method of feeding and the type of food provided are important, as is the following:

♚ A repotted bonsai should not be fed for at least three weeks, until new roots have developed. The plant would be unable to make use of the nutrients and unused food might accumulate and damage the new roots.

♚ Check that the potting mix is moist before applying a fertilizer. This helps spread the food evenly throughout the soil, as well as prevent root damage.

♚ Feed bonsai less frequently in winter than in summer. Inactive plants need less food than flowering ones.

♚ Weak concentrations of fertilizers are better than strong ones. Strong concentrations can build up in the soil and create a toxic environment for roots.

♚ If you are in doubt about which fertilizer to use, select one that is suitable for indoor bonsai and follow the manufacturer's instructions. It is better to gain confidence with one brand than to keep changing from one to another.

♚ Outdoor bonsai are exposed to rain that can leech nutrients from the soil. This problem does not normally affect indoor bonsai unless warm temperatures require you to water them more frequently.

Types of fertilizer

There are several different forms and applications of fertilizers:

❧ Fertilizers are available as liquid or solid. The latter includes powder, granules and pellets.

❧ Liquid fertilizers are diluted in water and applied at watering times. They become evenly spread throughout the soil and are easily absorbed by the roots.

❧ Powdered fertilizers are thoroughly mixed with water and are also applied at watering times. They are more likely to build up toxic residue in soil than those applied as liquids.

❧ Granular and pellet fertilizers are best added to the potting mix at repotting time. They are available to the roots over a long period, which may interfere with a plant's dormant or semi-dormant period, when little or no fertilizer is needed.

Organic or inorganic?

❧ Organic fertilizers, those derived from plant or animal substances, are not available to roots until broken down in the potting mix by microorganisms. They become available over a long period and do not create high salt concentrations in the potting mix that could damage roots.

❧ Inorganic fertilizers, sometimes known as full-spectrum fertilizers, come in the form of salts applied in both liquid and solid form. The food value is immediately available to roots, but if used in high dosages the inorganic fertilizers may increase the salt level in the soil. Therefore, always use them in weak dosages.

Left: *Many gardeners and bonsai enthusiasts opt for feeding their plants organically. This is a natural way to feed plants as it does not radically increase the presence of damaging salts in the potting mix. There are several brands of organic foods available; always adhere to the manufacturer's instructions when using them.*

Caring for your indoor bonsai

The main influences on the growth and health of your indoor bonsai are light, temperature and humidity.

Light

The position of a room invariably dictates the amount of light available to a plant. A sun-facing position provides the strongest and best light, but may be too intense for some plants. Throughout "The A to Z of Bonsai" (pp. 88–144) the intensity of light needed for each plant is described.

Do not position plants too close to a window, as the intensity of light may burn even those plants that like strong sunlight.

Temperature

Indoor bonsai vary in their required temperatures (also influenced by the intensity of light), and whereas *Buxus harlandii* (Harland boxwood) needs a winter temperature of 41–64°F (5–18°C), the *Carmona retusa* (Fukien tea) enjoys one up to 70°F (21°C). (Details of desired temperatures are given for each species detailed on pp. 88–144.)

Humidity

Indoor bonsai are tropical or subtropical plants and therefore welcome a humid atmosphere. Indeed, if the air is excessively dry there is a risk of leaves and flowers shriveling. The appropriate level of humidity depends on the temperature: the hotter it is, the higher the humidity should be in order to keep plants healthy. You can create humidity in two ways:

- Many indoor bonsai welcome having their leaves sprayed with a fine mist of clean water when the weather is warm. However, do not spray plants in strong or direct sunlight, and do not spray flowers.

- An alternative way to create humidity is to position several indoor bonsai in a shallow, non-draining tray that has been filled with wet gravel. Moisture rising from the gravel will provide humidity, as will the microclimate created when a number of plants are grouped together. A grouping of bonsai will require less artificial humidity than a solitary plant.

Below: *Gravel and pea shingle have a natural texture and color, and are used to create additional humidity around indoor bonsai. Ensure the tray does not leak water onto polished wood surfaces.*

Artificial light

Before you choose and install artificial light consider the following:

- Most forms of artificial light not only illuminate indoor bonsai, but encourage their healthy growth. The exception is tungsten-filament lights (also known as incandescent light bulbs). Their heat scorches leaves and flowers and causes houseplants to flower out of season – not desirable with indoor bonsai.

- Fluorescent tubes are the least expensive artificial lights and are available in several lengths, the most popular of which is 4 feet (1.2 m). Choose 40-watt types and, where two tubes are used, choose either two Grow Lux brand tubes or a combination of one "daylight" and one "cool-white" type. The choice and installation of lights varies from one country to another. However, generally they are best installed in a reflector that directs light downward onto plants.

- When illuminating indoor bonsai solely grown for their attractive foliage, position the lights about 1½–2 feet (45–60 cm) above the leaves. For flowering plants this can be decreased to 1 foot (30 cm). Check daily for scorch marks to ensure that the lights are not too close to the plants.

- Install a timer device that turns the lights on and off so that plants receive rays for about 14 hours a day. Do not exceed this period, as plants need a rest from active growth.

- The installation of lights that stimulate growth means plants need to be watered more frequently. Check that they are being sufficiently fed and provide a gentle circulation of air around the leaves with a thermostatically controlled electric fan. Ensure the air is not aimed directly at the plants and that the temperature is set at the average requirement (*see* pp. 88–144 for details for some specific species). Adequate humidity is also very important. To maintain the correct levels stand the plants in shallow waterproof trays filled with moist sharp sand.

- Employ a competent electrician to install all lights and ensure that regular safety checks are done.

Right: *Light bulbs are frequently used as a form of artificial lighting in display areas in nurseries, but they do not spread light as evenly as tube lights.*

Dealing with pests and diseases

Just like other plants, indoor bonsai can be attacked by pests and diseases. Always be vigilant and check leaves and flowers every time you water or prune to ensure that they are not punctured, chewed or covered by fungus. The earlier pests and diseases are treated, the less damage will occur to the plant and the easier it will be to eradicate the problem.

When buying a new plant, check it thoroughly. Inspect above and under the leaves and flowers. If the plant is infected but you still want to buy it, isolate it when you get home and treat it with a pesticide or fungicide. Usually, plants bought from reputable suppliers will be free from pests and diseases.

Spraying a plant

Take care to choose a suitable pesticide or fungicide. Check that it is recommended for indoor plants and, specifically, bonsai.

- Carefully identify the problem.
- Read the label and check that the product is suitable before using it.
- Do not use chemicals from unlabeled bottles. Never guess at the contents.
- Always follow the manufacturer's instructions — using extra high concentrations may damage plants.
- Keep children and pets out of the room while spraying. Birds and fish are sensitive to insecticides and pesticides.
- Don't allow pets to chew or lick sprayed plants.
- Thoroughly clean spray equipment after use.
- Don't spray near polished surfaces.
- Ventilate the room well when spraying is complete.

If you accidentally swallow or have an accident with a pesticide or fungicide, seek help immediately from a doctor. Take along the relevant spray.

Routine spraying

Prevention is easier than having to spray an infested plant. From early spring to late summer, spray at monthly intervals with a systemic insecticide and fungicide. Check your plants every day, especially a few weeks before you take a vacation — this provides time to eradicate an infestation.

Left: *Regularly spraying bonsai throughout the year — and especially during summer when insects are most active — helps to prevent minor infestations developing into epidemic proportions. Try to use chemicals sold especially for use on bonsai, such as the one being used on this* Diospyros whyteana *(bladdernut).*

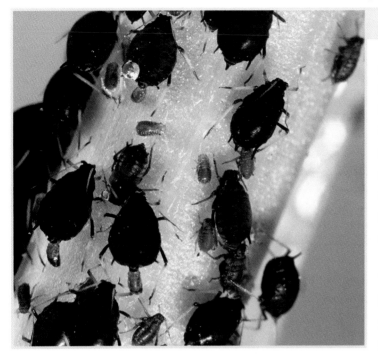

Aphids

Also known as greenfly, these pests are pernicious and wide-spread. They cluster around soft stems, young shoots and on the undersides of leaves, sucking sap, causing mottling and blistering, as well as transmitting viruses. If an infestation is severe, aphids excrete a sticky substance known as honey-dew, which attracts molds (usually black and known as sooty mold). For plants that are outdoors during summer, the honey-dew also attracts ants. There are many different species of aphids, with a wide color range.

Treatment: As soon as aphids are seen, spray plants with an insecticide. Repeat sprays are usually necessary. In addition, you can carefully wipe the leaves with a soft, damp cloth to remove sooty mold.

Blackfly

Similar to aphids, these pests cluster on soft stems, leaves and around the tender tips of shoots, sucking sap and trans-mitting viruses. Additionally, they excrete honeydew, which encourages the presence of ants as well as sooty mold. They are mostly seen on bonsai that are put outside during sum-mer. Although adult blackflies are usually distinctively black, when young and at certain times of the year they are green.

Treatment: As soon as they are seen, spray plants with an insecticide; repeat sprayings are usually necessary. Additionally, carefully wipe the leaves with a soft, damp cloth to remove sooty mold.

Caterpillars

Caterpillars are voracious eaters and soon damage soft shoots and leaves. Damage is worse during hot, dry summers. They are not common indoors, but are often present outdoors and in greenhouses and solariums.

Treatment: Pick off and destroy caterpillars, or spray with an insecticide. Ensure that the compost is moist. Where possible, remove badly damaged leaves to improve the plant's appearance.

Mealy bugs

These indoor plant pests resemble small woodlice covered in a white, mealy wax. They cluster around leaf joints, stems and leaves and, if ignored, form large colonies. They suck sap and excrete honeydew, which encourages the presence of sooty mold. Mealy bugs love warmth, which is why this pernicious pest is commonly found indoors or in greenhouses.

Treatment: Light infestations can be wiped off with cotton swabs dipped in methylated spirits or rubbing alcohol. Large colonies are best sprayed with an insecticide and wetting agent, to enable it to penetrate their waxlike covering.

Red spider mites

These spiderlike creatures, also known as greenhouse red spider mites, are barely visible to the unaided eye and vary in color from a transparent yellow white, through green to orange and brick red. In winter, their color tends to be red. Both adult and immature mites pierce and suck the undersides of leaves, causing a fine mottling on the upper leaf surface that becomes yellow and blotched if the attack is severe. Sometimes the mites create webs.

Treatment: Mist spraying reduces the risk of an infestation developing into epidemic proportions, but avoid wetting flowers and soft-textured leaves. Spray with an insecticide as soon as damage is noticed.

Root mealy bugs

Closely related to mealy bugs, this pest infests roots rather than leaves and stems. This impedes the growth of the plants, and causes foliage to wilt and discolor. Untreated plants die. Inspect the roots of plants when they are being repotted.

Treatment: If a plant shows the above symptoms, remove the pot and check the roots. If root mealy bugs are present, use a systemic insecticide to drench the roots and root ball. Repeat this several times, at 10- to 14-day intervals.

Scale insects

These insects are known to attack both outdoor and indoor plants. The first sign of infestation is when a plant becomes sticky. Swollen, waxy-brown discs can be seen on stems, branches and leaves, and it is under the leaves that female scale insects produce their young. They suck sap, causing debilitation in the plant and encouraging the presence of sooty mold. Severe infestations cause leaves to speckle and yellow.

Treatment: Young scale insects at the crawler stage are easy to kill and can be removed by being wiped with a cotton swab dipped in methylated spirits or rubbing alcohol. Large and well-established colonies are difficult to remove; use a systemic insecticide.

Slugs and snails

These are not usually pests of indoor plants, but can be a problem if bonsai are put outside during summer as they chew and tear leaves, stems and roots. Snails are especially fond of wet and warm weather. They hide during the day and are active at night; their presence is often indicated by trails of slime. These pests are able through smell to detect the presence of soft, young shoots and leaves.

Treatment: Where possible, raise plants above ground level to make them difficult to reach. Put down slug baits, or saucers of sugar and beer that will lure and trap them. Remove dead slugs and snails each morning and ensure that family pets and wild animals cannot reach the slug bait.

Thrips

Thrips infest plants in solariums, sunrooms and greenhouses; they are not major pests outdoors but if indoor bonsai are put outside in summer they may be attacked. The tiny dark brown flylike insects have light-colored wings and jump from plant to plant where they feed by piercing and sucking sap from the leaves and flowers, causing silvery mottling and streaking. In severe infestations, flowers become distorted and the undersides of leaves display small globules of red liquid that eventually turn black.

Treatment: As soon as thrips are noticed, spray plants several times with a systemic insecticide.

Vine weevils

Both the larvae and adult beetles damage plants. Adults chew and tear leaves, while larvae feed on roots. Attacks on leaves are soon seen, but root damage is only noticeable when the plant wilts. When repotting, check that the soil is free from small, legless (usually curved) creamy white grubs. The beetles are characterized by their dark bodies covered in short hairs.

Treatment: Pick off and destroy the larvae and beetles. Where potting mix is contaminated, soak it with an insect-icide. The beetles are most active at night.

Whitefly

These small white mothlike flies infest many soft-tissued indoor plants in greenhouses and solariums. When disturbed they flutter from plant to plant. Their young green nymphs are found mainly on the undersides of leaves where they suck sap and excrete honeydew. This encourages the presence of sooty mold. The leaves of an infected bonsai turn yellow, become black and messy through sooty mold and eventually fall off. Some plants, such as *Fuchsia magellanica* (hardy fuchsia) and *Punica granatum* var. *nana* (dwarf pomegranate), are especially susceptible to attack.

Treatment: It is not easy to eradicate whitefly. Repeatedly spray at three- or four-day intervals for a couple of weeks.

Woolly aphids

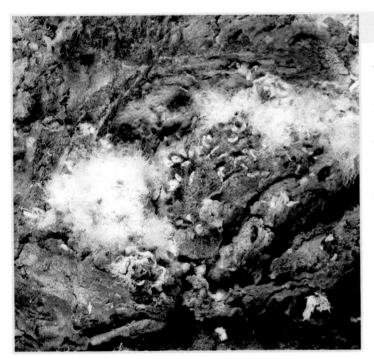

These occasionally infest indoor bonsai put outside in summer. Aphidlike insects produce masses of white, wool-like wax that covers and protects them. They often cluster around the junctions of stems and branches, sucking sap and causing the plant to be unsightly.

Treatment: Small colonies can be carefully wiped off with a cotton swab soaked in methylated spirits or rubbing alcohol. Alternatively, use a systemic insecticide.

Common diseases

Powdery mildew

This fungal disease affects the surfaces of leaves, coating and spotting them with an unsightly white powdery deposit. It also infects stems and flowers. It is not a fatal disease, but one that causes owners of bonsai great distress.

Treatment: Spray leaves with a systemic fungicide. Increasing the circulation of air around a plant with the aid of a thermostatically controlled electric fan helps to prevent the presence of powdery mildew. Ensure the air is not blowing directly onto the leaves and that the temperature is set at the correct level.

Sooty mold

Sooty mold lives on honeydew excreted by a wide range of sap-sucking insects, including aphids and scale insects. Leaves and flowers become smothered with the black mold. At first, the deposit appears in small clusters, but soon spreads and merges until the entire surface is covered.

Treatment: Spray sap-sucking insects as soon as they − or the results of their presence − are seen. Additionally, wipe away light infestations with a damp cloth.

Chapter 4

A to Z of Bonsai

Bonsai are long-term plants that often become treasured parts of a home environment, whether it be a house in a suburb or a high-rise apartment in the city. There are many indoor and outdoor bonsai featured in this chapter, all of which are incomparably fascinating.

This section elaborates on each plant's cultural prerequisites. These include style of growth and care instructions, and guidance on how to begin converting them into a bonsai. This may involve buying an established bonsai, modifying a small and inexpensive plant bought from a garden center or specialist nursery, or raising a plant from cuttings and seeds.

Some of the species included will present a challenge to enthusiastic bonsai hobbyists, but have been included because their biological features indicate a suitability for bonsai. The icons that appear with each species denote the most suitable styles for each individual plant (*see* pp. 38–41). Plants have been designated as "indoor" or "outdoor" in the directory based on the following criteria:

Indoor Bonsai Mainly created from tropical and subtropical plants. In temperate and colder climates they need to be grown indoors throughout the year, although in mild areas they can be put outside on warm and sheltered patios.

Outdoor Bonsai Created from winter-hardy trees, shrubs, conifers (evergreen and deciduous) and climbers. They are usually left outdoors throughout the year, although some would need shelter in exceptionally cold climates.

Temperature variations within North America range from the near subtropical and frost-free conditions in southern Florida to exceptionally cold conditions at higher latitudes. It is therefore impossible to indicate the treatment for each species in all areas of North America. Indications of temperatures are given in the text, but if you are unsure about putting a bonsai outdoors in winter contact your local bonsai nursery or club.

Opposite: *You can create a well-spaced network of branches, such as on this* Acer buergerianum *(trident maple) by wedging different lengths of chopsticks into neighboring branches or by using wire to shape the branches. (Artist: Kyuzo Murata)*

Styles to consider

Getting started

- Buy an established indoor bonsai.
- Buy a houseplant and modify it into an indoor bonsai (*see* pp. 28–35).
- Take lengths of 3 inch (7.5cm) half-ripe cuttings in mid-summer; insert them in equal parts moist peat and sharp sand in a propagating frame at a minimum temperature of 70°F (21°C). (*See* pp. 26–27 for details.)

Bougainvillea glabra
Bougainvillea

Paper flower

A woody climber, the bougainvillea is native to Brazil and features insignificant white flowers surrounded by spectacular bracts in various shades of red and purple. It can be cultivated as a deciduous or semi-deciduous plant depending on how the temperature is regulated indoors. Although a climber, when grown as an indoor bonsai it forms a thick trunk.

Looking after your plant

Position and temperature

During summer, place the plant in a bright sunlit room. In winter, a temperature of 45–54°F (7–12°C) is essential; avoid direct strong sunlight.

Watering and misting

Keep the soil moist during spring and summer, especially when plants are flowering. Mist spray plants throughout summer, but not when they are in direct sunlight. Throughout autumn and winter, keep the soil barely moist.

Feeding

Use a weak liquid fertilizer every 10 to 14 days from late spring to late summer.

Pruning and training

Prune in autumn after the plant has finished flowering and continue into winter. Pruning is also possible during summer, but do not touch the flowers. Established mature growth is brittle so do not reshape it with wires.

Soil and repotting

Well-drained potting mix is essential. Repot in early spring before fresh growth appears. Do not repot more frequently than every three or four years.

Buddleja indica

Earlier known as *Buddleia indica* and *Nicodemia diversifolia*, this evergreen shrub from Madagascar is a climber. As an indoor bonsai it forms a neat shrub. The leaves, which are especially attractive when young, are shiny green and slightly pear shaped. Sometimes the plant bears small pale yellow to yellow-green flowers.

Looking after your plant

Position and temperature

During summer place the plant outdoors in a warm wind-sheltered area, but avoid strong direct sunlight. In winter bring the plant indoors, but avoid high temperatures at night.

Watering and misting

During summer keep the soil moist, but not waterlogged. Water less in winter especially if the bonsai is in a cool room, but do not allow the soil to dry.

Feeding

Use a weak liquid fertilizer at two- to three-week intervals during summer, but only every four weeks in winter, especially if the room is cool.

Pruning and training

Young plants are much easier to shape than old ones, therefore start pruning and training them at a young age.

Soil and repotting

Well-drained potting mix is essential. Repotting is necessary every two years to replenish soil and to trim back the roots.

Styles to consider

Artist: Rudi Adams, Buddleja saligna

Getting started

- Buy an established indoor bonsai.
- Buy a young potted plant from a garden center and modify it into an indoor bonsai (*see* pp. 28–35).
- Take lengths of 4 inch (10 cm) half-ripe cuttings, with heels, in midsummer and insert them in equal parts moist peat and sharp sand in a cold frame (*see* pp. 26–27).

Styles to consider

Getting started

- Buy an established indoor bonsai.
- Buy a young potted plant from a garden center and modify it into an indoor bonsai (*see* pp. 28–35).
- Take hardwood cuttings 3–4 inches (7.5–10 cm) long in late summer or early autumn and insert them in equal parts moist peat and sharp sand in a cold frame (*see* p. 27).

Buxus harlandii
Harland boxwood

Box

Native to southern China and Hong Kong and earlier confused with *Buxus microphylla* 'Sinica' or *Buxus sinica*, this slightly tender evergreen shrub needs warmth and protection when grown in temperate and cold climates. It can be easily killed or severely damaged by frost. The bark is corky, yellow-brown and deeply furrowed. The leaves are shiny, pale green and in the shape of long narrow spoons. The small light green to yellow flowers cluster around leaf joints and create added color from spring into summer.

Looking after your plant

Position and temperature

During summer put your plant outside in a warm, lightly shaded and wind-protected position. In winter put it in a bright sunny position indoors at a temperature of 41–64°F (5–18°C). Avoid strong direct sunlight.

Watering and misting

At each watering thoroughly soak the soil. In winter water less frequently, but do not allow the soil to become dry.

Feeding

From late spring to late summer apply a weak liquid fertilizer every three to four weeks. In winter feed only once or twice, and only if the plant is growing strongly.

Pruning and training

You can prune and wire throughout the year. Ensure the wires do not cut into the bark and cause damage.

Soil and repotting

Use well-drained potting mix, and ensure that it is not acidic. This can be checked with a pH soil-indicating kit; the reading should be slightly above pH 7.0. Repot your plant in spring, before new growth appears, every two or three years.

Camellia japonica
Common camellia

A popular evergreen shrub hardy in temperate regions, except for its flowers that are damaged by late-winter and early-spring frosts. It is native to Japan, China, Korea and the Liu Kiu Islands. The thick, shiny dark green leaves create an attractive background for the flowers — single- and double-flowered forms — that are white through pink and red to purple.

Looking after your plant

Position and temperature

During summer place your indoor bonsai outdoors in a warm, sheltered and slightly shaded position. In early autumn move the bonsai indoors, initially giving it a cool position, but later slowly increasing the temperature by a few degrees. Do not expose it to high or fluctuating temperatures, and once it is ready to flower do not move it.

Watering and misting

During summer keep the soil consistently moist. In winter, keep it slightly drier, but once buds appear increase the amount of water. Mist spray plants but avoid wetting the flowers.

Feeding

Throughout summer feed plants with a weak liquid fertilizer every two or three weeks.

Pruning and training

After the flowers fade and during summer plants can be pruned. Wiring can be performed throughout the year except from late autumn or early winter and until the flowers fade.

Soil and repotting

Well-drained, acid potting mix at a pH reading of about 6.5 is essential. Repot your plant when its container becomes packed with roots, usually every four or five years. However, when plants are young and growing strongly repot them every two years.

Styles to consider

Getting started

- Buy an established indoor bonsai.
- Sow seeds in spring or early summer in acid potting mix using pots or seed trays. Avoid high temperatures — a warm or cool greenhouse is best.
- Buy a young potted plant from a garden center and modify it into an indoor bonsai (*see* pp. 28–35).
- Take half-ripe cuttings 3–4 inches (7–10 cm) long during summer, and insert them in equal parts moist peat moss and sharp sand. Place them in a propagating frame at a minimum of 55–61°F (13–16°C) (*see* pp. 26–27 for details).

Styles to consider

Getting started

- ✂ Buy an established indoor bonsai.
- ✂ Sow seeds in spring in seed trays at a temperature between 61–64°F (16–18°C). (*See* pp. 19–21 for details.)
- ✂ Take half-ripe cuttings 3–4 inches (7.5–10 cm) long in midsummer; insert them in equal parts moist peat moss and sharp sand in a propagating frame at a minimum temperature of 61°F (16°C). (*See* pp. 26–27 for details.)

Carmona retusa
Fukien tea

Philippine tea

Earlier known as *Carmona microphylla*, *Carmona heterophylla*, *Ehretia buxifolia* and *Ehretia microphylla*, this evergreen shrub is native to a wide area from India to Malaysia and the Philippine Islands. It has small dark green glossy leaves and in early summer bears white flowers, followed by green berries that turn red.

Looking after your plant

Position and temperature

In warm areas, place outdoors during summer in a lightly shaded, wind-sheltered position, or keep it indoors throughout the year. If kept indoors throughout summer, avoid hot spots where the soil can become warm. In winter, a temperature of 54–70°F (12–21°C) is desirable.

Watering and misting

Keep the soil consistently moist throughout summer, but in winter ensure it is barely moist. You will damage the plant, however, if you allow the soil to become dry. Lightly mist spray plants in summer.

Feeding

From spring to early autumn feed every two weeks with a weak liquid fertilizer. In winter feed your plant every four or five weeks, but only if it is in a warm position and shows moderate growth.

Pruning and training

From spring to late summer regularly trim back new shoots to two or three leaves. Only use wire to train trees when they are young and the stems are pliable.

Soil and repotting

Well-drained potting mix is essential. Repot young plants every two years in spring. Older, well-established plants can be left for four or five years. These plants do not like a radical reduction in their root size; all that is necessary is to cut off the outer roots from the root ball.

Citrus limon
Lemon

This is a small evergreen tree native to southeast Asia, but it is now widely grown in the Mediterranean and other warm regions. It is rarely grown in the tropics, however, where lime predominates. Lemon leaves are shiny and oval with tapering points. The variegated lemon has green and cream leaves and is often grown as an indoor bonsai.

Looking after your plant

Position and temperature

During summer put the plants outdoors in a sunny wind-protected position. In winter provide a steady even temperature of 46–55°F (8–13°C).

Watering and misting

Throughout summer keep the soil moist; several waterings a day may be necessary if the temperature is high. In winter keep the soil barely moist. During summer regularly mist spray plants, but not if they are in strong direct sunlight.

Feeding

From spring to early autumn feed your plant every two weeks with a weak liquid fertilizer. Do not feed plants in winter when they are partially dormant.

Pruning and training

Prune young shoots when they are pliable. Thicker shoots can be pruned at any time, but late spring throughout summer is best. Take care when wiring as the branches are often brittle.

Soil and repotting

Well-drained acid soil at a pH reading of about 6.5 is essential. Repot plants in spring, every three or four years, but take care not to inflict damage on the roots.

Styles to consider

Getting started

- Buy an established indoor bonsai (occasionally possible).
- Buy a small plant, grown as a houseplant, and modify it into an indoor bonsai (*see* pp. 28–35).
- Sow pits in summer. Plants cultivated this way are slow to grow, may not resemble the parent, or may not flower for many years (*see* pp. 19–21).
- Take half-ripe cuttings 3–4 inches (7.5–10 cm) in mid- and late summer; insert them in equal parts moist peat and sharp sand in a propagating frame at a temperature of 61–64°F (16–18°C). (*See* pp. 26–27 for details.)

Styles to consider

Getting started

- Buy an established bonsai.
- As soon as the seeds are ripe in autumn sow them in pots and place in a cold frame.
- Take heel cuttings in late summer and place in a cold frame.

Cotoneaster horizontalis
Fishbone cotoneaster

Rockspray

Cotoneaster is normally evergreen. In countries with temperate climates it is a hardy, low-growing deciduous shrub with leaves that are oval, glossy and dark green and arranged on branches that resemble fish bones. Initially, it grows horizontally, then later upright. It produces small pink flowers in early summer followed in autumn by rich red berries that persist throughout most of winter.

Looking after your plant

Position and temperature

In summer position the plant in full sunlight. Although it is a hardy shrub, protect it from cold winds in winter as they can damage the ends of the branches.

Watering

Water sparingly all year. Cotoneasters naturally grow in rocky mountainous areas and hate having wet roots.

Feeding

Use half-strength balanced fertilizer in spring and low nitrogen from midsummer until autumn.

Pruning and training

Cotoneasters are extremely dense and need regular trimming throughout the summer. In early spring, further thinning can be carried out and branches can be pruned. Exposing new wounds to frost can cause drastic dieback of the surrounding bark.

Wire at any time during summer when the bonsai is growing strongly.

Soil and repotting

Repot your bonsai every one or two years when it is young; later, every two or three years when roots fill the pot. Use well-drained potting mix.

Crassula arborescens
Chinese jade

Chinese jade plant, jade plant, jade tree, money tree, silver jade plant

Earlier known as *Crassula cotyledon* and now often classified as *Crassula atropurpurea* var. *arborescens*, this evergreen slow-growing perennial, native to the Western Cape, South Africa, has sturdy branches and thick fleshy gray-green leaves. In its native area it produces small starlike white flowers maturing to pink-red, but in temperate climates these are seldom seen.

Looking after your plant

Position and temperature

Keep the plant indoors throughout the year, with a minimum winter temperature of 50°F (10°C) not exceeding 64°F (18°C). In summer the temperature will rise higher, but as this is accompanied by better light, it does not matter. Position the plant near a sunny window.

Watering and misting

During summer keep the soil lightly moist, but not wet. In winter water less, but do not allow the soil to become dry. The lower the temperature the less water is needed. Mist spraying is not necessary.

Feeding

From mid-spring to early autumn give your plant a weak liquid fertilizer every four or five weeks. Do not feed your plants during winter.

Pruning and training

Prune at any time of the year and cut off crossing branches. Wiring is seldom needed.

Soil and repotting

Well-drained potting soil is essential. Repot every three or four years in spring. Do not radically cut off roots: about 10 percent of the root ball is right.

Styles to consider

Getting started

- Buy an established indoor bonsai.
- Buy a young houseplant and modify it into an indoor bonsai (*see* pp. 28–35).
- Take leaf cuttings in spring and summer. Detach a leaf by pulling or bending it off from an established plant and leave it to dry for a day. Insert the broken end of the leaf into a mixture of one part slightly moist peat and two parts sharp sand. Firm the mix around the bases of each cutting (*see* p. 27 for details). The broken ends will produce roots; you can then repot the cuttings.

Styles to consider

Crassula ovata
Jade plant

Baby jade plant, cauliflower ears, Chinese rubber, dollar plant, dwarf rubber, jade tree, Japanese rubber

Earlier known as *Crassula argentea* and *Crassula portulacea*, this succulent multibranched shrub is native to the Western Cape, South Africa, and is widely seen outdoors in other warm areas, such as California. It develops green leaves that are flattened yet succulent. They are pear shaped and shiny with red edges. Slowly, after about two or three years, the plant develops a thick, gnarled light fawn trunk.

Looking after your plant

Position and temperature

Keep the plant indoors throughout the year at a minimum winter temperature of 50°F (10°C) not exceeding 64°F (18°C). In summer, the temperature will rise higher, but as this is accompanied by better light it does not matter. Position the plant near a sunny window.

Watering and misting

During summer keep the soil lightly moist, but not wet. In winter water less, but do not allow the soil to become dry. The lower the temperature the less water is needed. Mist spraying is not necessary.

Feeding

From mid-spring to early autumn give a weak liquid fertilizer every four or five weeks. Do not feed plants during winter.

Pruning and training

Prune at any time of the year and cut off crossing branches. Wiring is seldom needed.

Soil and repotting

The use of well-drained potting mix is essential when repotting every three or four years in spring. Do not radically cut off roots: about 10 percent of the root ball is right.

Getting started

- Buy an established indoor bonsai.
- Buy a young houseplant and modify it into an indoor bonsai (*see* pp. 28–35).
- Take leaf cuttings in spring and summer. Detach a leaf from an established plant by pulling or bending, and leave it to dry for a day. Insert the broken end of the leaf into a mix of one part slightly moist peat and two parts sharp sand. Firm the mix around the bases of each cutting, which will later grow roots. The leaf cutting can then be repotted (*see* pp. 22–23 and 25).

Crassula sarcocaulis

A dwarf shrubby succulent from South Africa, this *Crassula* has woody stems and small pointed green leaves, which are often flushed red, especially during summer. From midsummer to early autumn, it bears pink flowers, but with an unpleasant aroma. There is also an attractive white-flowered form.

Looking after your plant

Position and temperature

Keep the plant indoors throughout the year at a minimum winter temperature of 50°F (10°C), not exceeding 64°F (18°C). In summer, the temperature rises higher, but as this is accompanied by better light it does not matter. Position the plant near a sunny window.

Watering and misting

During summer keep the soil lightly moist. In winter water less, but do not allow the soil to dry. The lower the temperature the less water is needed. Mist spraying is not necessary.

Feeding

From mid-spring to early autumn give a weak liquid fertilizer every four or five weeks. Do not feed plants during winter.

Pruning and training

Prune at any time of the year; cut off crossing branches. Wiring is seldom needed.

Soil and repotting

The use of well-drained potting mix is essential. Repot every three or four years in spring. Do not radically cut off roots: about 10 percent of the root ball is about right.

indoor plant

Styles to consider

Getting started

- Buy an established indoor bonsai.
- Buy a young houseplant and modify it into an indoor bonsai (*see* pp. 28–35).
- Take leaf cuttings in spring and summer. Detach each leaf from an established plant by pulling or bending it off and leave it to dry for a day. Insert the broken end of the leaf into a mix of one part slightly moist peat and two parts sharp sand. Firm the mix around each base. The broken ends later produce roots and the leaf cuttings can be repotted. (*See* pp. 22–23 and 25.)

Styles to consider

Cryptomeria japonica
Japanese cedar

Japanese red cedar, temple cedar

This evergreen conifer has bright orange-brown peeling bark and needlelike bright blue-green leaves that are curved and dagger shaped. There are several forms, such as 'Tansu' (also known as 'Yatsubusa'), which is compact and small with a narrow conical shape, making it ideal as a bonsai.

Looking after your plant

Position and temperature

Position the plant in full sun. In winter shelter the plant from cold wind.

Watering

Water evenly in order to keep the soil constantly just damp.

Feeding

Feed with a weak liquid fertilizer every two or three weeks from mid-spring to late autumn.

Pruning and training

Prune branches in autumn. Trim shoots to keep the tree as neat as is required, and then thin out the congested areas toward the middle of summer.

Wire during summer or autumn after pruning. Wire may have to be reapplied several times before thicker branches set.

Soil and repotting

Repot your bonsai every one or two years when it is young; later, every two to four years when roots fill the pot. Use well-drained potting mix.

Getting started

- Buy an established bonsai.
- Take softwood cuttings in summer.

Cycas revoluta
Japanese sago palm

False sago, sago palm

A primitive plant with a palmlike appearance native to southern Japan and the Ryukyu Islands, Japanese sago palm is not a true palm. It is slow growing and evergreen, often growing just one rosette of leaves a year. In the wild it forms a beautiful rose of stiff arching foliage, but when grown as a bonsai this is seldom seen.

Looking after your plant

Position and temperature

This plant requires warmth throughout the year and needs to be kept indoors at a temperature not below 59°F (15°C). Bright light is essential, but not strong direct sunlight. Rapidly fluctuating temperatures and differences in light intensity will damage the plant.

Watering and misting

Keep the soil moist during summer. In winter reduce the frequency of watering, but never allow the soil to become dry. Only mist spray plants in summer, but ensure they are not in direct sunlight.

Feeding

Apply a weak liquid fertilizer every four weeks during summer, but only a couple of times in winter when the plant is less active.

Pruning and training

Little pruning is needed. Wiring can be used to shape the leaves when young. Once mature, wiring is not needed and the leaves will hold their desired position.

Soil and repotting

Only repot your *Cycas* when the potting mix is congested (every five or six years for established plants). When they are young and growing strongly repotting every two years might be necessary.

Styles to consider

Getting started

- Buy an established indoor bonsai.
- Sow seeds in spring or early summer in seed trays in a greenhouse at a temperature of 70–80°F (21–27°C). Both germination and subsequent growth are slow — up to three months for germination (*see* pp. 18–21).
- Detach small bulbs (suckerlike offsets) from the plant and position them in a propagating frame at 24–82°F (75–28°C). Insert them shallowly in equal parts moist peat and sharp sand. It is best to do so in late spring and throughout summer.

indoor plant

Styles to consider

Getting started

- Buy an established indoor bonsai.
- Buy a houseplant and modify it into an indoor bonsai (*see* pp. 28–35).
- Sow seeds in spring or early summer in pots or seed trays at 61–64°F (16–18°C) (*see* pp. 18–21 for details).
- Take cuttings 2–4 inches (5–10 cm) long from lateral shoots from mid-spring to early summer; insert them in equal parts moist peat and sharp sand in a propagating frame at 61–64°F (16–18°C) (*see* pp. 25–27 for details).

Ficus benjamina
Java fig

Benjamin tree, small-leaved rubber plant, tropical laurel, waringin, weeping fig, weeping laurel

A popular evergreen shrub native to a wide area including south and southeast Asia, through to Malaysia and northern Australia and the southwest Pacific, the Java fig is grown as a house and office plant because of its grace. It has slender pendulous side branches with soft green leaves that become darker with age. There are several forms with variegated or narrow leaves.

Looking after your plant

Position and temperature

Keep your plant indoors throughout the year. In winter 59°F (15°C) is best, while during summer the temperature will rise naturally. Avoid rapidly fluctuating temperatures as this may cause leaves to fall off. Avoid strong direct sunlight during summer.

Watering and misting

Keep the soil evenly moist throughout summer. In winter water less frequently but do not allow the soil to become dry as this, together with low temperatures, may cause leaves to fall off. Mist spray leaves throughout summer, but not when they are in strong sunlight.

Feeding

Every two or three weeks throughout summer use a weak liquid fertilizer. In winter feed at four- to five-week intervals.

Pruning and training

Prune your plant throughout the year. However, because it grows more actively in summer, you may need to prune more then. Wire throughout the year, but avoid cutting into the bark.

Soil and repotting

Well-drained potting mix is essential. Repot throughout the year, but preferably in spring, as summer temperatures encourage rapid root growth.

Ficus carica
Brown turkey fig
Common fig, fig, fig tree

This deciduous shrub is native to a wide area from Cyprus, Turkey and Caucasia to Turkestan and Afghanistan. It is one of the oldest cultivated plants and known for its three- or five-lobed shiny green leaves and succulent fruits. Although the leaves are normally large, when plants are repeatedly pruned and encouraged to produce more branches, the size of the leaves diminishes gradually and can eventually be dramatically reduced.

Looking after your plant

Position and temperature
In summer place outdoors in a sunny and sheltered position. From mid-autumn to late spring it needs a cool and bright position indoors.

Watering and misting
During summer keep the soil moist but not waterlogged. In late autumn or early winter the leaves fall off, and once this happens, keep the soil barely moist. If too much water is given at this stage the roots will start to decay. During summer mist spray leaves, but not if the plant is in strong direct sunlight.

Feeding
From late spring to early autumn give the plant a weak liquid fertilizer every 10 to 14 days. Older plants do not require regular feeding. Do not feed during winter and early spring.

Pruning and training
Start pruning in spring by cutting back growth of the previous season. Throughout summer cut back new growth for the development of small leaves. Wires can be used to shape the branches.

Soil and repotting
Well-drained potting mix is essential. Repot young plants every two or three years and established ones every four to six years, and then only if the pot is packed with roots. Giving a fig plant too much fresh potting mix encourages lush rapid growth.

Styles to consider

Getting started

- Buy an established indoor bonsai.
- Take half-ripe cuttings with heels 4–5 inches (10–13 cm) long in late summer or early autumn, and insert them in equal parts moist peat and sharp sand in a cold frame (*see* pp. 26–28 for details).

Styles to consider

Getting started

- Buy an established indoor bonsai.
- Buy a houseplant and modify it into an indoor bonsai (*see* pp. 28–35).
- Take cuttings 2–4 inches (5–10 cm) long from lateral shoots from mid-spring to early summer; insert them in equal parts moist peat and sharp sand in a propagating frame at 61–64°F (16–18°C). (*See* pp. 25–27 for details.)

Ficus lingua
Box-leaved fig

Earlier known as *Ficus buxifolia*, this evergreen shrub is native to a wide area of Africa, from Mozambique to Kenya and Uganda and across central Africa to Cameroon and west Africa. It has small slightly triangular green leaves that are blunt and slightly rounded at their tips. Occasionally flowers grow from the leaf joints followed by small green inedible fruits that become red-brown.

Looking after your plant

Position and temperature

It is best kept indoors throughout the year. In winter, provide a minimum temperature of 50°F (10°C). During summer, the temperature will rise, but as long as it is not too high and accompanied by good light, the plant will thrive.

Watering and misting

Keep the soil evenly moist during summer, but when the temperature falls in winter water your plant less frequently. Mist spray the leaves in summer, but not when the plant is in strong direct sunlight.

Feeding

From late spring to early autumn apply a weak liquid fertilizer every two or three weeks. Feed your plant every four or five weeks during winter, but only if it is growing actively.

Pruning and training

Prune your plant from late spring to early autumn, shaping branches and cutting them back as necessary. You can wire young branches. Take care with older branches as they are inflexibile and you could damage their bark.

Soil and repotting

Well-drained potting mix is essential. Repot in spring when the roots fill the pot; repot young plants every two years and established plants at three- or four-year intervals.

Ficus microcarpa
Banyan fig

Chinese banyan, curtain fig, glossy-leaf fig, Indian laurel, laurel fig, Malay banyan

Earlier known as *Ficus retusa*, this evergreen spreading shrub is native to southern China, south and southeast Asia, Australia and the Pacific Islands. The tough, oval to broadly elliptic glossy green leaves create a canopy, while inedible berries, initially green then purple and black, arise from leaf joints. In the wild, *Ficus microcarpa* produces masses of aerial roots. As a bonsai its roots cluster around the trunk.

Looking after your plant

Position and temperature

During summer place plants outdoors in a bright sunny position. In winter, however, a room temperature of 64–75°F (18–24°C) is required. Position the plant in good light and avoid cold drafts.

Watering and misting

Throughout summer keep the soil evenly moist. If it is too dry or moist the leaves may drop off. In winter take care to not moisten the soil excessively. Mist spray the foliage, but not when the plant is in strong sunlight.

Feeding

From late spring to early autumn feed plants every two to three weeks with a weak liquid fertilizer. During winter feed them only once every four weeks.

Pruning and training

Prune plants mainly in spring or early summer and cut off unwanted branches.

Soil and repotting

Well-drained potting mix is essential. Repot young plants every two or three years and older plants when their roots become congested in their containers.

Styles to consider

Getting started

- Buy an established indoor bonsai.
- Buy a houseplant and modify it into an indoor bonsai (*see* pp. 28–35).
- From mid-spring to early summer take cuttings 2–4 inches (5–10 cm) long from lateral shoots; insert them in a propagating frame in equal parts moist peat and sharp sand at 61–64°F (16–18°C). (*See* pp. 25–27 for details.)

Styles to consider

Ficus natalensis
Natal fig

This evergreen shrub from tropical and southern Africa has many pear-shaped dark green leaves. In less tropical areas, the plant can be semi-deciduous. It is relatively hardy and adapts well to life indoors.

Looking after your plant

Position and temperature

During summer, place this fig outdoors in a warm, wind-sheltered area. It grows well in direct sunlight, but needs to be slowly acclimatized to high-intensity light. In winter, bring the plant indoors at a room temperature of 64–75°F (18–24°C).

Watering and misting

Keep the soil moist throughout summer. In winter take care not to waterlog the soil. Mist spray plants throughout summer, but not when they are in strong sunlight.

Feeding

From mid-spring to early autumn feed the plant every two or three weeks with a weak liquid fertilizer. If it is growing strongly, feed every four to five weeks during winter. If exposed to high temperatures you may need to feed more frequently.

Pruning and training

Although you can train your plant into several styles, you'll find the broom style (*see* p. 40) the easiest to achieve through radical pruning. To achieve other styles you may need to wire the branches, but do not do so if the plant is older than three years.

Soil and repotting

Keep the potting mix well drained. Repot young plants that are growing strongly every two years, and older ones only every three or four years, when their roots fill the containers.

Getting started

- Buy an established indoor bonsai.
- Buy a houseplant and modify it into an indoor bonsai (*see* pp. 28–35).
- From mid-spring to early summer take cuttings 3–4 inches (7.5–10 cm) long; insert them in a propagating frame in equal parts moist peat moss and sharp sand at 61–64°F (16–18°C). (*See* pp. 25–27 for details.)

Ficus religiosa
Peepul

Bo tree, Sacred fig tree

A deciduous or semi-deciduous tree from the Himalayan foothills to southwest China, northern Thailand and Vietnam. A specimen has been found dating back to 288 B.C. The tree is venerated by Buddhists and Hindus. The heart-shaped and wavy-edged leaves are normally large, but with repeated pruning they decrease in size. It bears inedible fruit that turns dark purple when ripe.

Looking after your plant

Position and temperature
Throughout winter place your plant in a very warm and humid room. If the air is dry and the temperature high its leaves will fall off. During summer place your bonsai outdoors. Ensure it is protected from the wind and direct sunlight.

Watering and misting
In summer lightly moisten the soil. In winter do not saturate the soil, especially when cold.

Feeding
From mid-spring to mid-autumn feed your plant with a weak liquid fertilizer every two or three weeks. In winter feed every four or five weeks.

Pruning and training
Prune regularly during summer. Once leaves reach a length of 4–5 inches (10–15cm), cut new shoots back to one to three leaves. You can train young branches by wiring, but ensure the wires do not cut into the bark.

Soil and repotting
Use well-draining potting mix. Repot a young plant annually in spring, but an older one only when its roots fill the container.

Styles to consider

Getting started

- Buy an established indoor bonsai.
- Buy a houseplant and modify it into an indoor bonsai (*see* pp. 28–35).
- Sow seeds in spring or early summer in temperatures of 61–64°F (16–18°C). (*See* pp. 18–21 for details.)
- From mid-spring to early summer take cuttings 2–4 inches (5–10 cm) long; insert them in a propagating frame in equal parts moist peat moss and sharp sand at 61–64°F (16–18°C). (*See* pp. 25–27 for details.)

Styles to consider

Getting started

- Buy an established indoor bonsai.
- Buy a houseplant and modify it into an indoor bonsai (*see* pp. 28–35).
- From mid-spring to early summer take cuttings 2–4 inches (5–10 cm) long; insert them in a propagating frame, in equal parts moist peat and sharp sand, at 61–64°F (16–18°C). (*See* pp. 25–27 for details.)

Ficus rubiginosa
Botany Bay fig

Little-leaf fig, Port Jackson fig, rusty fig, rusty-leaved fig

This small evergreen tree, native to the Australian state of New South Wales, has elliptic glossy dark green leaves covered with rust-colored down (*see* p. 149). Buttressing roots add further interest to the tree. There is a beautiful form called 'Variegata' with leaves variegated green and creamy yellow.

Looking after your plant

Position and temperature

In summer put the plant outside in a warm, wind-sheltered position. During winter you must grow the plant indoors. Position it in bright light at a temperature above 50°F (10°C). Avoid exposing it to fluctuating temperatures.

Watering and misting

Throughout summer and winter keep the soil moist. Avoid saturating the roots, however. Mist spray the leaves, but not when the plant is in strong direct sunlight.

Feeding

From late spring to early autumn feed plants every three weeks with a weak liquid fertilizer. Throughout winter feed every four or five weeks.

Pruning and training

Prune regularly throughout summer. Cut new shoots back to outward-facing buds. Train young branches by wiring them, but ensure the wires do not cut into the bark.

Soil and repotting

Use well-draining potting mix. Repot young plants every two years in spring and older plants only when their roots fill the pot.

Ficus salicifolia
(F. cordata var. salicifolia)
Willow-leaved fig

Now known as *Ficus cordata* var. *salicifolia*, this evergreen shrub is native to tropical Africa, southern Algeria, Libya and Egypt. It is also known on the Socotra Island and the southern Arabian Peninsula. The long and narrow spear-shaped leaves are rich dark green and form a dense canopy. The plant bears berries that are initially green and later become red or purple-brown.

Looking after your plant

Position and temperature

During summer place the plant outdoors in a warm, wind-sheltered position away from strong direct sunlight. In winter place it in a warm, highly humid room. Once returned indoors, willow-leaved fig will lose its leaves, although it is evergreen in the wild.

Watering and misting

In summer when there is increased leaf growth, keep the soil moist but take care not to waterlog it. Excessive water at this stage will damage the roots. When the plant sheds its leaves in winter decrease the amount of water.

Feeding

From late spring to early autumn feed your plant every two or three weeks with a weak liquid fertilizer. In winter feed every four or five weeks, but only if the plant has many leaves.

Pruning and training

The broom is the easiest bonsai style to achieve (*see* p. 40) because this plant produces masses of leaves. You can wire it if you wish.

Soil and repotting

Keep the potting mix well drained. Repot young plants every two years, and established plants every three or four years.

Styles to consider

Getting started

- Buy an established indoor bonsai.
- Buy a houseplant and modify it into an indoor bonsai (*see* pp. 28–35).
- From mid-spring to early summer take cuttings 2–3 inches (5–7.5 cm) long; insert them in a propagating frame, in equal parts moist peat and sharp sand, at 61–64°F (16–18°C). (*See* pp. 25–27 for details.)

Styles to consider

Getting started

- Buy an established indoor bonsai (occasionally possible).
- Buy a small houseplant and modify it into an indoor bonsai (*see* pp. 28–35).
- Sow pits in summer. Plants cultivated this way are slow to grow, may not totally resemble the parent, or may not flower for many years (*see* pp. 19–21 for details).
- In mid- and late summer take half-ripe cuttings 3–4 inches (7.5–10 cm) long; insert them in a propagating frame in equal parts moist peat and sharp sand at 61–64°F (16–18°C). (*See* pp. 26–27 for details.)

Fortunella hindsii
Dwarf kumquat

Dwarf orange, Hong Kong kumquat, Hong Kong wild kumquat

A tender evergreen shrub from Hong Kong and China, dwarf kumquat has oval, glossy deep green leaves and small white fragrant flowers. If the temperature and humidity are high, the plant may produce fruits that ripen to a flame orange.

Looking after your plant

Position and temperature

During summer put the plant outdoors in a warm and sunny wind-protected position. In winter provide a steady and even room temperature of 46–55°F (8–13°C).

Watering and misting

In summer if the temperature is high, you may need to water the soil moderately several times a day. Regularly mist spray the leaves if the plant is in strong direct sunlight. Keep the soil barely moist in winter.

Feeding

From spring to early autumn feed your plant every two weeks with a weak liquid fertilizer. Do not feed plants in winter when they are partially dormant.

Pruning and training

Prune young shoots when they are young and pliable. You can prune thicker shoots any time, although doing so in late spring and throughout summer is best. Take care when wiring as branches are often brittle.

Soil and repotting

Ensure the potting mix is well drained and that it has a pH reading of approximately 6.5. Repot plants every three or four years in spring, but take care to not inflict damage to the roots.

Gardenia jasminoides
Cape jasmine

Cape jessamine, common gardenia, gardenia, jasmine

Earlier known as *Gardenia augusta*, *G. florida* and *G. grandiflora*, this tender evergreen shrub from China, Taiwan and Japan is famed for its intensely fragrant flowers, especially the double-flowered forms. The leaves are glossy green and lance shaped, while the flowers appear at leaf joints from early to late summer.

Looking after your plant

Position and temperature

Keep your plant indoors throughout the year. Ensure it is at a constant room temperature of 54-59°F (12-15°C), and away from strong direct sunlight and drafts.

Watering and misting

Throughout summer keep the soil moist, especially when the plant is flowering. Mist spray plants, but avoid wetting the flowers. During winter water less frequently.

Feeding

From late spring to autumn feed your plant every 10 to 14 days with a weak liquid fertilizer, but not when the plant is flowering. Do not feed during winter.

Pruning and training

Prune plants at any time of the year, but not when they are flowering. Prune young shoots back to two or three leaves. You can wire throughout the year, but it is best to wait until after the flowers have faded.

Soil and repotting

Keep the potting mix well drained. Only repot plants in spring when their containers are packed with roots.

Styles to consider

Getting started

- Buy an established indoor bonsai.
- Buy a houseplant and modify it into an indoor bonsai.
- Sow seeds in spring or early summer in seed trays in 61-64°F (16-18°C). (*See* pp. 18-21 for details.)
- In spring take cuttings 3 inches (7.5 cm) long, preferably with a heel, from non-flowering shoots. Insert them in a propagating frame in equal parts moist peat and sharp sand at 64-70°F (18-21°C). When the cuttings have grown roots, transfer them to pots and reduce the room temperature.

Styles to consider

Getting started

- Buy an established bonsai.
- Sow seeds in pots as soon as they are ripe in mid-autumn, and place in a cold frame.

Ginkgo biloba
Maidenhair tree

This deciduous conifer grows slowly and has fan-shaped light green leaves with two lobes that darken in summer. In autumn, they turn pale yellow. The fissured dark gray bark is especially attractive. *Ginkgo biloba* trees vary in shape; the male trees are shaped like pyramids, whereas the female trees in Europe are tall and narrow.

Looking after your plant

Position and temperature

Do not place the plant in strong light in summer, especially when the leaves are young. In winter, position it in a wind-sheltered corner. To protect it from frost, place it under a slatted screen.

Watering

During summer water generously and keep the potting mix slightly moist in winter.

Feeding

Do not feed your bonsai excessively and when you do, use organic fertilizers. It is essential to use well-drained yet moisture-retentive soil.

Pruning and training

Prune branches in autumn or late winter. Prune the shoots as necessary to keep the tree neat throughout summer. Be sure to leave at least a small piece of stump in order to prevent dieback.

Wire in the summer, after the first growth has been established. Check the wires regularly and carefully remove all those that appear to be getting too tight.

Soil and repotting

Young maidenhair trees benefit from being repotted annually. After 10 years, once they have matured, repot every three years or when roots fill the pot. Always use well-drained, moisture-retentive potting mix.

Juniperus californica
Californian juniper

A tender evergreen native to California and the Baja Peninsula, this conifer is rugged with ridged gray-brown bark that flakes easily and scalelike yellow-green leaves. Native Americans used to gather the berrylike cones to eat fresh or to grind into meal for baking.

Looking after your plant

Position and temperature
During summer in mild areas, place your plant outside in a warm, wind-sheltered position. The plant also does well indoors in summer, in a cool but sunny position. In winter avoid strong direct sunlight and maintain a temperature of 45–54°F (7–12°C).

Watering and misting
During summer keep the soil moist but not saturated. Throughout winter less water is needed. Mist spray plants throughout summer, especially when the temperature is high.

Feeding
In summer feed your plant every two or three weeks with a weak liquid fertilizer. In winter feed only every four or five weeks if the temperature is high and the plant is growing actively.

Pruning and training
Leaf-prune branches throughout the year by pulling leaves out. This thins the leaves out rather than merely reshape them the way cutting does. You can wire throughout the year, but it is best to do so in summer.

Soil and repotting
Keep your potting mix well drained. Repot your plant every three or four years.

Styles to consider

Getting started

- Buy an established indoor bonsai.
- Buy a houseplant and modify it into an indoor bonsai (*see* pp. 28–35).
- Sow seeds as soon as they are available in seed trays at 68–75°F (20–24°C). (*See* pp. 19–21 for details.)

Styles to consider

Juniperus chinensis
Chinese juniper

This is an evergreen conifer with a conical shape and pale red-brown bark. Young leaves are short and needle shaped, and are scaly and a dull dark green once the plant matures. The foliage oozes resin when bruised. There are several forms of this plant, some small with gold leaves.

Looking after your plant

Position and temperature

During summer position the plant in full sun. In winter, place it under a slatted cover to protect it from cold winds and frost, which can damage the needles.

Watering

Throughout summer and winter keep the soil moist. In winter, avoid letting it dry out as this will damage the foliage.

Feeding

Apply a balanced fertilizer from spring until late summer. Continue to feed, at one-quarter strength, in winter if the tree is still growing.

Pruning and training

Prune branches in autumn or late winter. Constantly pinch out growing tips throughout the growing season. Cut the fatter extending shoots back to healthy side shoots to keep the vigor of the tree in check.

Wire at any time, provided the weather remains mild. Remove wire and reapply as necessary every six months.

Soil and repotting

Repot your bonsai every one or two years when it is young; later, every three or four years or when roots fill the pot. Use well-drained potting mix.

Getting started

⊗ Buy an established bonsai.
⊗ Sow seeds in pots in autumn and place in a cold frame.
⊗ Take cuttings in late summer or early autumn and place in a cold frame.

Juniperus rigida
Needle Juniper

Styles to consider

This is an elegant evergreen conifer with slender needlelike leaves that are yellow-green and prickly. In its second year of growth, the plant bears many green berries that ripen to purple-black. The trunk is sculpted and appears aged.

Looking after your plant

Position and temperature

During summer position the plant in full sun. In winter place it under a slatted cover to protect the needles from strong cold winds and frost.

Watering

Water moderately year round to keep the soil moist but not saturated.

Feeding

Feed moderately with a balanced fertilizer throughout the growing season. Overfeeding results in weak, sappy growth.

Pruning and training

Prune branches in autumn. Cut growing shoots back to two or three buds as they grow in summer. The buds form at the base of each needle.

Wiring can be done at anytime, but autumn and winter are best, provided the weather remains mild. Remove the wire every six months and reapply when necessary.

Soil and repotting

Repot your bonsai every two years when young; later, every three or four years or when roots fill the pot. Always use well-drained potting mix.

Getting started

- Buy an established bonsai.
- Sow seeds in pots in autumn and place in a cold frame.
- Take cuttings in late summer or early autumn and place in a cold frame.

Styles to consider

Lagerstroemia indica
Crape myrtle

Crepe myrtle, Chinese crape myrtle, crepe flower

This deciduous subtropical shrub from China, Indochina, the Himalayas and Japan has bark mottled with pink, cinnamon and gray that occasionally flakes. The oval leaves are first red and later green and mauve. Lilac flowers appear in late summer.

Looking after your plant

Position and temperature

In summer place your plant outdoors in a warm, shaded and wind-sheltered position, or indoors in direct sunlight. In winter remove the plant from direct sunlight and maintain a room temperature of 45–54°F (7–12°C).

Watering and misting

Keep the soil moist throughout summer, especially when the plant has its canopy of leaves. Take care not to saturate the soil during winter. At this stage, the plant is inactive and excessive moisture would damage the roots. In spring, as plant growth resumes, increase the amount and frequency of watering. Mist spray plants in summer, but avoid wetting the flowers.

Feeding

From spring, after growth resumes, use a weak liquid fertilizer every two weeks until three weeks before flowers form. (You will notice the flower buds.) Do not feed during winter.

Pruning and training

Prune in late autumn after the plant has flowered or in early spring before leaves develop. Flowers form at shoot ends and few flowers will appear if you have pruned them prematurely. Wire from late spring to midsummer — do not constrict the branches unnecessarily as this could damage them.

Soil and repotting

Use well-drained potting mix and repot every two or three years in spring, before growth begins.

Getting started

- Buy an established indoor bonsai, but these are difficult to obtain.
- Buy an established potted plant and modify it into an indoor bonsai (*see* pp. 28–35).
- In spring or early summer sow seeds at a temperature of 61–64°F (16–18°C). (*See* pp. 18–21 for details.)
- In late summer take 3-inch (7.5 cm) cuttings. Insert them in a propagating frame in sandy potting mix at a temperature of 61–64°F (16–18°C). (*See* pp. 25–27.)

Lantana camara
Lantana

Large-leaf lantana, shrubby verbena, yellow sage

Lantana is an evergreen shrub from tropical regions in the
Americas often grown as a houseplant in temperate climates.
The pale to dark green oval leaves often appear too large for a
bonsai, but regular pruning reduces their size. Domed heads of
tubular flowers develop from leaf joints in summer. There are
several forms in colors from white through to yellow and red. As
the flowers age they assume different colors.

Looking after your plant

Position and temperature

During summer place your plant outside in a warm,
wind-sheltered place, or leave it indoors in a sunny position. In
winter return your plant indoors and position it in a spot at a
temperature of 45˚F (7˚C). Later, in early spring, increase the
temperature to 50˚F (10˚C) or fractionally higher.

Watering and misting

In summer keep the soil moist, especially when the plant is flowering. Use less water in winter but do not allow the soil to dry.
Mist spray leaves in summer, avoiding the flowers.

Feeding

From spring to early autumn feed every two weeks with a weak
liquid fertilizer. In winter feed every four or five weeks.

Pruning and training

In autumn and spring radically cut back long stems to the main
branches. Young growth will develop; again cut back the stems
severely when they are about 6 inches (15 cm) long. This
encourages more shoots to develop that will bear flowers. Wire
only young branches.

Soil and repotting

Use well-drained potting mix. Repot plants in late winter, every
two or three years.

Styles to consider

Artist: John Naka
Lantana *sp.*

Getting started

- Buy an established indoor bonsai.
- Buy a young houseplant and modify it into an indoor
  bonsai (*see* pp. 28–35).
- In late summer take 3-inch (7.5 cm) cuttings from young
  shoots. Insert them in a propagating frame in equal parts
  moist peat and sharp sand at a temperature of 61–64˚F
  (16–18˚C). Transfer rooted cuttings to individual pots (*see*
  pp. 25–27); later pinch out the growing tips several times
  to encourage bushiness.

Styles to consider

Getting started

- Buy an established indoor bonsai.
- Buy a young potted plant and modify it into an indoor bonsai (*see* pp. 28–35).
- Sow fresh seeds at a temperature of 61–64°F (16–18°C). (*See* pp. 18–21 for details.)
- In midsummer take half-ripe cuttings 2–2½ inches (5–6 cm) long. Insert them in a propagation frame in equal parts moist peat and sharp sand at a temperature of 61°F (16°C). Transfer rooted cuttings to individual pots (*see* pp. 26–27).

Leptospermum scoparium
Manuka
New Zealand tea tree, South Sea myrtle, tea tree

A slightly tender evergreen shrub native to New Zealand and New South Wales, Victoria and Tasmania, Australia, manuka has narrow lance-shaped blue-green leaves. Clusters of pink or white flowers appear in early summer. There are several varieties in other attractive colors. It is not an easy plant to grow and often has a short lifespan as an indoor bonsai.

Looking after your plant

Position and temperature
Provide a cool and bright position throughout the year. Avoid high temperatures, especially in winter. In summer you can place it outdoors in a cool, wind-sheltered position in good light.

Watering and misting
During summer keep the soil evenly moist, especially when flowers are present. In winter water the plant less, but do not allow the soil to dry as this will damage the plant severely. Mist spray the foliage but avoid wetting the flowers.

Feeding
From late spring to early autumn feed your plant every two or three weeks with a weak liquid fertilizer. In winter feed the plant every four or five weeks, but only when it is producing new growth.

Pruning and training
Prune young plants severely in spring, but once they are established do not prune them until after they flower. You can wire young branches, but leave older ones alone because they are brittle.

Soil and repotting
Use well-drained acid potting mix with added peat moss. If the plant is growing strongly, repot only every one or two years. The tree is sensitive to root disturbance so it is important to repot very gently.

Ligustrum japonicum
Japanese privet
Wax-leaf privet

An evergreen shrub from Japan and Korea, Japanese privet is hardy in all climates but the severest of winters. It is also ideal for indoor bonsai owners with little experience. It has lustrous dark green leaves and clusters of white flowers that appear in mid and late summer.

Looking after your plant

Position and temperature
Place the plant outside in a warm, wind-sheltered position during summer. In autumn, before any risk of frost, return the plant indoors to a cool and bright room to keep foliage intact. Avoid high temperatures during winter.

Watering and misting
During summer keep the soil evenly moist. In winter reduce the amount and frequency of watering. There is no need to mist spray the leaves.

Feeding
From late spring to late summer feed your plant every two or three weeks with a weak liquid fertilizer. In winter extend this to every five or six weeks, especially if the plant is inactive.

Pruning and training
Prune young plants radically; cut back new shoots to three or four pairs of leaves. You can wire young branches that are up to two years old, but take care to not mark the bark.

Soil and repotting
Keep potting mix well drained. Repot every two years.

Styles to consider

Getting started

- Buy an established indoor bonsai.
- Buy a young potted plant from a garden center and modify it into an indoor bonsai (*see* pp. 28–35).
- In late summer take hardwood cuttings 4–6 inches (10–15 cm) long; insert them in pots of equal parts moist peat and sharp sand; place in a cold frame (*see* p. 27).

Styles to consider

Ligustrum sinense
Chinese privet

This is a shrub that is deciduous in excessively cold winters, but evergreen in mild ones. It has pale green leaves that are either lance shaped or oval. It bears white flowers in midsummer, followed by round, black-purple fruits that often persist through to the following year. This plant can also be grown indoors in cold climates.

Looking after your plant

Position and temperature

During summer position the plant in full sun. In winter, place it under a slatted screen to protect it from cold winds and frost. Alternatively, in very cold areas, place the bonsai in a cold room in good light.

Watering

Water often, but only if the soil feels dry.

Feeding

Feed with balanced fertilizer in summer, and at one-quarter strength in winter if buds are still opening.

Pruning and training

Prune at any time. Trim new shoots to one pair of leaves throughout the growing period. Thin out overcrowded areas and cut away adventitious shoots several times a year.

Wire at any time. If you should snap a thin branch while wiring, it should survive and mend itself within a year or so, provided at least half the branch is still intact. Privet grows shoots at all angles, so branch shaping can be done by pruning alone.

Soil and repotting

Repot your bonsai annually when it is young; later, every other year or when roots fill the pot. Use well-drained yet moisture-retentive potting mix. The fine feeding roots regenerate with great rapidity, so prune the roots quite thoroughly each time you repot.

Getting started

- Buy an established bonsai.
- Take cuttings in late summer or early autumn and place them in a cold frame.

Malpighia coccigera
Singapore holly
Dwarf holly, miniature holly

A small, often prostrate, evergreen shrub from the West Indies, dwarf holly has pear-shaped, glossy pale green leaves with spine-toothed edges. Pink or lilac flowers appear in summer, followed by small and round red berries. It is not easy to grow this plant as an indoor bonsai, and it needs great care to ensure longevity.

Looking after your plant

Position and temperature
During summer give your plant a bright, but lightly shaded position indoors. If you live in an area with a mild climate you can put your plant outside in a warm, shaded and wind-protected position. If you live in a region with a temperate or cooler climate, you must keep your plant indoors in winter at a temperature of 68°F (20°C), or slightly above, and increase the humidity in the room to match the rise in temperature.

Watering and misting
Throughout the year keep the soil evenly moist. Dramatic variations in soil moisture can cause the plants to lose their leaves. Mist spray regularly and shade it from direct sunlight.

Feeding
From late spring to mid-autumn feed your plant every three or four weeks with a weak liquid fertilizer. In winter do so every five weeks, but only if the plant is showing signs of growth.

Pruning and training
Prune the shoots back to two or three leaves when they are about 4 inches (10 cm) long. Wire your plant when it is young and its shoots are supple.

Soil and repotting
Ensure the potting mix is well drained. Repot established plants every two or three years. Repot young plants every two years.

Styles to consider

Getting started

- Buy an established indoor bonsai.
- Buy a young potted plant from a garden center and modify it into an indoor bonsai (although plants are only available occasionally).
- In summer take half-ripe cuttings 3–4 inches (7.5–10 cm) long. Insert them in a propagating frame in equal parts moist peat and sharp sand at a temperature of 64°F (18°C). (*See* pp. 26–27 for details.)

Styles to consider

Malus spp.
Crab apple

This is a hardy deciduous tree with glossy green leaves that are oval and bowl shaped. It bears clusters of slightly fragrant flowers during spring, followed by round fruits that resemble small apples. There are many superb species and varieties available. The apples ripen in autumn and range in color from yellow to red.

Looking after your plant

Position and temperature

During summer, provide the plant with full sun. In winter, place it in a frost- and wind-sheltered area to protect the roots. Ensure the plant has good light.

Watering

Water copiously in spring and summer, less in winter. Always ensure that the soil is moist when the plant is flowering and bearing fruits.

Feeding

Feed with a weak liquid fertilizer every two weeks in early spring until the plant flowers; then every two or three weeks until early or mid-autumn, after the fruits have developed.

Pruning and training

Prune branches in autumn if necessary. Cut back last year's shoots to a convenient bud after flowering. Allow subsequent growth to flourish freely until late summer, then cut back, leaving between two and four buds. Remember that the buds at the base of each shoot are next year's flower buds.

Wire in summer to build a basic branch arrangement. Develop heavy branches by pruning, rather than by wiring.

Soil and repotting

Repot your bonsai every year when it is young; later, every two or three years or when roots fill the pot. It is essential to use well-drained yet moisture-retentive potting mix.

Getting started

✂ Buy an established bonsai.
✂ Grafting is the usual method of propagation.

Murraya paniculata
Chinese box

Cosmetic bark tree, orange jasmine, orange jessamine, satinwood

Native to a wide area — China, India and Australia — this tender evergreen tree has smooth light brown bark, bright green leaves and clusters of jasminelike, fragrant white flowers that appear throughout the year. After the flowers fade, inedible berries follow, which turn from orange to bright red.

Looking after your plant

Position and temperature

Keep your plant indoors throughout the year except if you live in a temperate region. In this case, you could put it outdoors in summer in a warm, wind-sheltered, lightly shaded position. During winter provide an approximate temperature of 55°F (13°C).

Watering and misting

Water the plant repeatedly throughout the year. In summer increase the frequency of watering. If you keep the soil well drained you cannot harm the plant.

Feeding

From spring to autumn feed every two weeks with a weak liquid fertilizer. If the room temperature is warm in winter and the plant is growing well, apply a liquid feed every four weeks. If the room temperature is low and the plant is inactive, cease feeding it.

Pruning and training

You can prune plants throughout the year, but take care as flower buds sprout on new growth. Wire plants during summer when they are growing actively; avoid damaging the trunk and branches with the wire.

Soil and repotting

Use well-drained potting mix. Repot your plant every two or three years.

Styles to consider

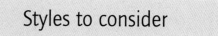

Getting started

ʃ Buy an established indoor bonsai.

ʃ Buy a young potted plant from a garden center and modify it into an indoor bonsai (*see* pp. 28-35).

ʃ In mid- to late summer take 3 inch (7.5 cm) half-ripe cuttings. Insert them in a propagating frame in equal parts moist peat and sharp sand at a minimum temperature of 76°F (24°C). (*See* pp. 26-27 for details.)

Styles to consider

Getting started

⊗ Buy an established indoor bonsai.

⊗ Buy a young potted plant from a garden center and modify it into an indoor bonsai (*see* pp. 28–35).

⊗ Sow seeds in spring or early summer in seed trays (*see* pp. 18–21).

⊗ In early or midsummer take cuttings 2–3 inches (5–7.5 cm) long with heels from non-flowering lateral shoots. Insert them in a propagating frame in equal parts moist peat and sharp sand at a room temperature of 61°F (16°C). (*See* pp. 25–27 for details.)

Myrtus communis
Common myrtle

Greek myrtle, Indian buchu

Myrtle is a tender evergreen shrub native to Mediterranean regions and southwest Europe. The oval leaves are glossy and pale to dark green with fragrant white flowers that bloom from early to late summer. Purple-black fruits may follow.

Looking after your plant

Position and temperature

During summer place your plant outdoors away from cold drafts in slight shade rather than strong direct sunlight. In winter provide a bright but cool position at a temperature of 41–45°F (5–7°C).

Watering and misting

Throughout summer, keep the soil moist when the plant is growing strongly. In winter, water less. Mist spray leaves throughout summer.

Feeding

From late spring to early autumn feed your plant every two weeks with a weak liquid fertilizer. Well-established mature plants need little feeding — one feeding every four or five weeks is quite sufficient. Do not feed your plant in winter when it is dormant.

Pruning and training

Prune annually in spring. Cut back shoots to either four or two pairs of leaves. It is not necessary to wire this plant when it is established, although you can shape its branches when it is young and growing actively.

Soil and repotting

Use well-drained potting mix. Repot your plant every two or three years in spring before new growth appears.

Nandina domestica
Sacred bamboo

Chinese sacred bamboo, Heavenly bamboo

An evergreen or semi-deciduous shrub native to India and eastern Asia, sacred bamboo has long and narrow pale green leaves that turn red in autumn and winter. It has a clump-forming nature (*see* p. 41). Occasionally, white florets develop in clusters from mid- to late summer. Bright red berries may follow. Although associated with bamboo, this plant is not bamboo but related to *Berberis* (barberry), a group of shrubs also of the Berberidaceae family.

Looking after your plant

Position and temperature

In summer you can either keep your plant indoors in bright but indirect sunlight, or outside in a warm, wind-sheltered spot shaded from strong direct light. In winter position your plant in bright light, ideally at a temperature of 45–55°F (7–13°C).

Watering and misting

Keep the soil moist throughout the year, but reduce the amount and frequency of waterings in winter when the plant is inactive. Mist spray the foliage in summer.

Feeding

Throughout summer feed your plant every two weeks with a weak liquid fertilizer. In winter feed every four or five weeks, but not if it is dormant.

Pruning and training

You can prune your plant any time of year. Cut back the shoots so they sit just above the soil. *Nandina domestica* does not produce many side shoots; it is best to cut back exceptionally tall stems level with the surface of the soil.

Soil and repotting

Use well-drained potting mix. Repot your plant every three or four years when its container is filled with roots.

Styles to consider

Getting started

- Buy an established indoor bonsai.
- Buy a young potted plant from a garden center and modify it into an indoor bonsai (*see* pp. 28–35).
- Sow seeds in late summer or early autumn in pots. Place them in a cold frame (*see* pp. 18-21 and 28).
- In early autumn take cuttings 3–4 inches (7.5–10 cm) long, with heels, from lateral shoots. Insert the cuttings in pots in equal parts moist peat and sharp sand. Place the pots in a cold frame. (*See* pp. 25–28 for details.)

Styles to consider

Getting started

- Buy an established indoor bonsai.
- Buy a young potted plant from a garden center and modify it into an indoor bonsai (*see* pp. 28–35).
- Sow seeds in spring or early summer in pots with sandy potting mix. Place the pots in a cold frame and maintain a temperature of 45°F (7°C) until the seeds germinate.
- In midsummer take 3-inch (7.5 cm) half-ripe cuttings with heels from established plants. Insert the cuttings in pots filled with equal parts moist peat and sharp sand. Place the pots in a cold frame (*see* pp. 26–27).

Olea europaea
Common olive

Edible olive

A slightly tender evergreen shrub with oval leaves that are shiny and dark green with gray undersides. The attractive light gray bark is one of the main features of this bonsai. The light cream or off-white flowers are followed by green fruits which ripen through red to purple-black.

Looking after your plant

Position and temperature

During summer you can put this plant outside in a wind-sheltered position. During winter, however, you must keep it indoors near a window in bright light at a temperature ranging from 46–64°F (8–18°C). Guard against high temperatures at night.

Watering and misting

During summer water the soil whenever it becomes dry, but take care not to drench it. In winter less water is needed as the plant is inactive. Mist spray the leaves throughout summer.

Feeding

Throughout summer, feed your plant every two or three weeks with a weak liquid fertilizer. In winter feed your plant only if it is producing new growth; every four or five weeks would be ideal. Feeding your plant any more than this will damage it.

Pruning and training

Prune your plant throughout the year. Allow young shoots to develop two or three pairs of leaves before cutting them back.

Soil and repotting

Use well-drained potting mix. Repot your plant every two or three years.

Pinus parviflora
Japanese white pine

Earlier known as *Pinus parvifolia* and *Pinus pentaphylla*, this hardy evergreen conifer develops a low crown with branches that spread widely and are packed with clusters of five blue-white needles. There are many forms, such as *Pinus parviflora* 'Kokonoe' (dwarf Japanese white pine), that are ideal for growing as a bonsai.

Looking after your plant

Position and temperature

During summer place the plant in full sunlight. In winter place it under a slatted screen to protect it from cold winds and frost.

Watering

Water moderately in the summer, sparingly in winter, and then only if necessary.

Feeding

Use low-nitrogen fertilizer until the new needles spread, then feed with high-nitrogen plant food until autumn.

Pruning and training

Prune branches in autumn. New shoots must be shortened (or cut off completely in congested areas) in midsummer. Let the new inner shoots gain strength for one or two years before cutting them away.

Wire in late summer and autumn.

Soil and repotting

Repot young bonsai every year; later, every three to five years or when roots fill the pot. Use well-drained potting mix.

Styles to consider

Getting started

- Buy an established bonsai.
- Sow fresh seeds in pots in early spring and place in a cold frame.

Styles to consider

Pinus thunbergii
Japanese black pine

This is a hardy evergreen conifer with bark that is deeply fissured. It has bright green leaves that are straight, stiff and upright; the plant bears them in pairs for three to five years. The branches are open and sparse. There are many forms of this conifer, whose physical appearance as bonsai differ vastly from their original counterparts.

Looking after your plant

Position and temperature

During summer place the plant in full sunlight. In winter place it under a slatted screen to protect it from cold winds and frost.

Watering

Water sparingly at all times, even less when the needles are maturing. Never allow the soil to become waterlogged.

Feeding

Feed with a low-nitrogen fertilizer while the shoots ("candles") are extending, then switch to high-nitrogen feed in late summer and autumn to encourage the production of plenty of new buds. Do not feed your plant excessively during winter.

Pruning and training

Prune branches in autumn or late winter. Pinch or cut off about two-thirds to three-quarters of each of the extending candles as the needles begin to peel away.

Wire in summer after removing old needles and pinching new candles. Shoots are flexible, but often short and thick, which makes fine adjustments difficult.

Soil and repotting

Repot young bonsai every year; later, every two to five years or when roots fill the pot. Use well-drained potting mix.

Getting started

- Buy an established bonsai.
- Sow fresh seeds in pots in early spring and place in a cold frame.

Pistacia lentiscus
Mastic tree

Chios mastic, Chios mastic tree, lentisc

Mastic tree is an evergreen shrub native to the Mediterranean region, except northeast Africa. It has variably shaped, but mainly oval, dark green shiny leaves. In the wild it produces flowers followed by inedible fruits that are initially red and later black. It produces gum that was used in early dentistry.

Looking after your plant

Position and temperature

During summer place your plant outdoors in a warm, wind-sheltered position. Introduce it first to filtered light and then slowly to bright light. In winter, or whenever the temperature falls outside, take your plant indoors and position it in bright light in a cool room not below 41°F (5°C).

Watering and misting

Water your plant moderately throughout the year, but take care not to overwater in winter as the plant is inactive then. Mist spray your plant during summer, but not if it is in strong direct sunlight.

Feeding

From late spring to early autumn feed your plant with a weak liquid fertilizer every 10 to 14 days. In winter extend this to every four or five weeks.

Pruning and training

Prune in spring when the plant is growing rapidly. Allow young shoots to grow 6–8 inches (15–20 cm) before cutting them back to either four, three or two leaves. New shoots will develop and you will need to prune these, too. Wire branches up to two years old, but check that the wires are not cutting into the bark.

Soil and repotting

Use well-drained potting soil and extra-sharp sand. Repot your plant every three or four years, when roots fill the pot.

indoor plant

Styles to consider

Getting started

- Buy an established indoor bonsai.
- Buy a young potted plant and modify it into an indoor bonsai (*see* pp. 28–35).
- In spring or early summer sow seeds in pots or seed trays at 61°F (16°C). (*See* pp. 18–21 for details.)
- In late summer take 3-inch (7.5 cm) half-ripe cuttings from an established plant. Insert them in a pot in equal parts moist peat and sharp sand. Place the pots in a cold frame. (*See* pp. 26–27 for details.)

Styles to consider

Getting started

- ✂ Buy an established indoor bonsai.
- ✂ In late summer, take 3-inch (7.5 cm) half-ripe cuttings. Insert them in pots in equal parts moist peat and sharp sand. Place the pots in a cold frame. (*See* pp. 26–28.)

Pistacia vera
Green almond

Fustuq, pistachio, pistachio nut

A spreading and tender deciduous tree native from Iran to central Asia and the eastern Mediterranean, green almond has oval leaves that are shiny and dark green with dull green undersides. Brown-green flowers appear in late spring followed by long, oval red fruits. In warm climates *Pistacia vera* produces pistachio nuts.

Looking after your plant

Position and temperature

During summer you can put your plant outside in a bright and sunny wind-sheltered area. In winter you must keep the plant indoors, in a bright position at a temperature above 50°F (10°C), although for short periods it can survive a minimum temperature of 45°F (7°C).

Watering and misting

Keep the soil evenly moist throughout the year. In winter, however, take care to not overwater the plant. Mist spray your plant in summer.

Feeding

From late spring to early autumn feed your plant every two weeks with a weak liquid fertilizer. In winter feed it every five or six weeks if the temperature is high and the plant is actively growing.

Pruning and training

You can prune throughout summer. Pinch back young shoots to create bushiness and maintain the small size of the plant. You can wire plants when they are growing well.

Soil and repotting

Use well-drained potting mix and extra-sharp sand. Repot your plant every three or four years when its roots fill the pot and after its flowers fade.

Podocarpus macrophyllus
Big leaf

Big-leaf podocarp, Buddhist pine, Chinese yew,
Chinese podocarpus, Kasamaki, Japanese yew,
podocarp, podocarpus yew, southern yew

Big leaf is a slow-growing evergreen conifer native to southern
China and Japan with distinctive narrow dark green leaves. The
trunk appears aged and its roots are exposed. The plant resembles the *Taxus baccata (*English yew) and is a member of the
Taxaceae or Podocarpaceae family. It is not sufficiently hardy to
be grown outdoors in temperate climates.

Looking after your plant

Position and temperature

During summer you can put your plant outside in a wind-sheltered, bright and warm position. In winter take the plant
indoors into a cool area, temperature of 41–45°F (5–7°C), away
from direct sunlight.

Watering and misting

During summer and winter keep the soil lightly moist and
mist spray the leaves, but not when the plant is in strong
direct sunlight.

Feeding

During summer feed your plant every two or three weeks with a
weak liquid fertilizer. In winter feed every five or six weeks.

Pruning and training

Prune at any time of the year. Allow new shoots to grow up to
3 inches (7.5 cm) before cutting them back. You can wire at
any time, but check regularly that the wires are not cutting
into the bark.

Soil and repotting

Use well-drained potting mix. Repot your plant every three or
four years at a minimum because it is slow growing. Lightly
prune back the roots.

Styles to consider

Getting started

- Buy an established indoor bonsai.
- Buy a young potted plant and modify it into an indoor
  bonsai (*see* pp. 28–35).
- Propagate a plant by means of seeds and cuttings.

Styles to consider

Getting started

⊗ Buy an established indoor bonsai.
⊗ Buy a young potted plant and modify it into an indoor
  bonsai (*see* pp. 28–35).

Portulacaria afra
Elephant bush
Purslane tree

A shrub native to South Africa, elephant bush has firm, fleshy
and near-horizontal branches that bear thick pear-shaped bright
green leaves, which store water. In South Africa it grows in arid
areas and is said to be deciduous in times of drought. You can
water an indoor bonsai throughout the year, however, and it
will not lose its leaves.

Looking after your plant

Position and temperature

In summer place your plant in a bright and sunny position
indoors. In extremely warm areas you can put it outside in
direct sunlight from early to late summer, but avoid cold
drafts. From autumn to late spring ensure the
plant is indoors in a bright position. Ensure
heating is turned off at night.

Watering and misting

In summer water the plant constantly. In winter only water
the plant once the surface of the soil starts to dry. No mist
spraying is needed.

Feeding

From late spring to early autumn feed your plant every two
weeks with a weak liquid fertilizer. From mid-autumn to mid-
spring, only feed your plant if it is in a warm room, then feed it
every four or five weeks.

Pruning and training

When shoots are 2 inches (5 cm) long, cut back growth to one
or two pairs of leaves. You can wire, but check that the wires do
not cut into the bark.

Soil and repotting

Use well-drained potting mix and add extra-sharp sand or fine
gravel. Repot established plants in spring when their roots fill the
containers, which usually occurs every three years.

Punica granatum var. *nana*
Dwarf pomegranate

Dwarf pomegranate is a small deciduous, sometimes semi-deciduous, branching shrub with oblong, glossy pale green leaves. In autumn they become light red. In late spring and early summer the tree produces red or white flowers followed by brown-yellow to purple-red fruits.

Looking after your plant

Position and temperature

Keep the plant indoors in bright light throughout the year. In summer the temperature rises naturally; in winter a minimum of 45°F (7°C) is essential. In warm areas you can put the plant outside in summer in a bright, wind-sheltered position.

Watering and misting

In summer keep the soil moist but not waterlogged. Water less in winter. Mist spray the foliage in summer, but not if it is in strong sunlight.

Feeding

From late spring to early autumn feed your plant every three weeks with a weak liquid fertilizer. Do not feed your plant in winter.

Pruning and training

If you are growing your plant for its flowers, cut back shoots severely once after the flowers have faded. The fresh shoots will bear flowers the following year. If you are solely focused on growing your plant for its foliage, prune it in spring. You can wire the branches.

Soil and repotting

Use well-drained potting mix. Repot your plant every one or two years when it is young, but less frequently when it is older. Do so after its leaves have fallen and just before new ones appear.

Styles to consider

Getting started

- Buy an established indoor bonsai.
- Buy a young potted plant from a garden center and modify it into an indoor bonsai (*see* pp. 28–35).
- Sow seeds in spring. Place them in a propagating frame at a temperature of 61°F (16°C). Later, transfer the seedlings to individual pots (*see* pp. 18–23).
- Take 3-inch (7.5 cm) half-ripe cuttings with heels in mid-summer. Insert the cuttings in equal parts moist peat and sharp sand in a propagating frame at 61–64°F (16–18°C). (*See* pp. 26–27 for details.)

Styles to consider

Getting started

⚮ Buy an established bonsai.
⚮ Take half-ripe cuttings in early summer; insert in pots of equal parts moist peat and sharp sand; provide gentle warmth.

Rhododendron indicum
Satsuki azalea

Sometimes known as *Azalea indica*, this low-growing and dense evergreen shrub has small, narrow dark green leaves. During early summer it becomes awash with either white, pink, red or purple flowers. Some plants have flowers with a mix of these colors; some are even blotched or speckled. There are many varieties of this plant, some of which have variegated leaves.

Looking after your plant

Position and temperature

During summer place the plant in dappled sunlight. In winter, place it under a slatted screen to protect it from cold winds, frost, rain and heavy falls of snow.

Watering

Satsukis won't tolerate dry roots, but they are not particularly thirsty. Water only when necessary, keeping the soil evenly moist all year round.

Feeding

Feed with a low-nitrogen fertilizer in the growing season. Always use an acidic ericaceous (lime-free) fertilizer.

Pruning and training

Prune branches and shoots in early summer, after flowering. Thin out dense areas to allow young inner shoots room to grow. Wire only in summer and only when you cannot prune for shape. Wire only young shoots until you become more experienced because the branches and older shoots break very easily.

Soil and repotting

Repot young bonsai every year; later, every two years or when the pot is full of roots.

Sageretia thea
Sageretia

Earlier known as *Sageretia theezans*, this tropical evergreen shrub from central and eastern China has small, oval-shaped and shiny green leaves that have shades of pink-brown when young. The trunk has smooth peeling bark with contrasting dark and light brown patches. White flowers sometimes appear, especially if the plant is not pruned regularly. Later, it may bear purple-black berries.

Looking after your plant

Position and temperature

You need to keep the plant indoors throughout the year, in a warm bright room away from direct sunlight. Do not allow the room temperature to fall below 50°F (10°C). In warmer temperate climates you can put the plant outside in summer, but only if the temperature is high and the plant is protected from cold wind.

Watering and misting

Keep the soil moist at all times, but in winter ensure that it does not become waterlogged. Regularly mist spray the leaves.

Feeding

Throughout summer feed your plant every two or three weeks with a weak liquid fertilizer. In winter apply a weak feed every five or six weeks, but only if the plant is actively growing.

Pruning and training

You can prune your plant at any time throughout the year, but in early spring is preferable. Cut back long shoots to one or two pairs of leaves. Wire only young shoots; old stems are difficult to manipulate and may snap.

Soil and repotting

Use well-drained potting mix. You only need to repot when roots fill the pot, at two- or three-year intervals.

Styles to consider

Getting started

⊗ Buy an established indoor bonsai.

⊗ Buy a young potted plant and modify it into an indoor bonsai (*see* pp. 28–35).

⊗ Take 3-inch (7.5 cm) half-ripe cuttings with heels in mid-summer. Insert the cuttings in equal parts moist peat and sharp sand in a propagating frame at a temperature of 61–64°F (16–18°C). (*See* pp. 26–27 for details.)

Styles to consider

Schefflera actinophylla
Australian ivy palm

Australian umbrella tree, octopus tree, Queensland umbrella tree, starleaf, umbrella tree

Earlier known as *Brassaia actinophylla* and *Schefflera brassaia actinophylla*, this slow-growing evergreen tree from north and northeast Australia and south and southeast New Guinea has shiny pale green leaves that form an umbrellalike arrangement. Mature plants usually have leaves formed of five leaflets, while young plants only have three. *Schefflera actinophylla* is grown as a houseplant in colder climates.

Looking after your plant

Position and temperature

Keep your plant indoors throughout the year, in bright light to encourage the leaves to remain small. In winter maintain the room temperature at 55°F (13°C).

Watering and misting

Keep the soil lightly moist throughout the year, especially during summer, and ensure you do not waterlog it in winter. Mist spray your plant during summer and winter, but not when it is in strong direct sunlight.

Feeding

From late spring to mid-autumn feed your plant every four weeks with a weak liquid fertilizer. During winter, especially if the temperature is low, feed your plant only every six weeks.

Pruning and training

This plant is slow growing and needs little pruning; only when a shoot gets too high and out of proportion with the rest of the plant is pruning necessary. When such a shoot is 6 inches (15 cm) too long, cut it back to encourage shoots lower down to develop. Wiring is not needed.

Soil and repotting

Use well-drained potting mix. Repot every two or three years, when the container is packed with roots.

Getting started

- Buy an established indoor bonsai.
- Buy a young potted plant from a garden center and modify it into an indoor bonsai (*see* pp. 28–35).

Serissa japonica
Tree of a thousand stars

This tender, densely branched evergreen shrub, earlier known as *Serissa foetida*, is native to Southeast Asia. It has lance-shaped, smooth dark green leaves that are foetid when crushed, as are the roots. The white flowers are usually single, but double-flowered forms are known, some of which have variegated leaves.

Looking after your plant

Position and temperature

During summer you can put your plant outside if the weather is warm and the area is sheltered from cold wind. In winter place the plant indoors in a bright position, and maintain a temperature of 50–68°F (10–20°C). Avoid strong direct sunlight.

Watering and misting

Keep the soil moist throughout summer, but slightly less in winter. Do not allow it to become dry. Mist spray the leaves, but not when the plant is in strong direct sunlight.

Feeding

During summer feed your plant every two or three weeks with a weak liquid fertilizer. In winter every four or five weeks is better.

Pruning and training

You can prune throughout the year, but doing so in early spring is best. Cut off dead flowers. It is best to wire during summer.

Soil and repotting

Use well-drained potting mix with extra-sharp sand. Repot your plant every two or three years, in spring before new growth appears.

Styles to consider

Getting started

- Buy an established indoor bonsai.
- Buy a small potted plant from a garden center or specialist grower and modify it into an indoor bonsai (*see* pp. 28–35).

Styles to consider

Stewartia monadelpha

Earlier known as *Stuartia monadelpha*, this hardy deciduous tree has smooth peeling bark. The leaves are oval and their fresh green color turns to shades of red and purple in autumn. The plant bears white flowers during mid- and late summer.

Looking after your plant

Position and temperature

During early and midsummer shade the plant from strong sunlight. In late summer and mid-autumn provide it with good light. In winter place the plants under a slatted screen in a sheltered corner to protect them from cold winds and frost.

Watering

Water diligently, keeping the soil moist at all times, but avoid waterlogging. Use only rainwater or lime-free tapwater.

Feeding

Use an ericaceous fertilizer, one that is balanced and made for acid-loving plants, throughout the growing season.

Pruning and training

Prune branches in autumn or early spring. Prune shoots back to one or two leaves. Keep the branch framework open to allow light and air to penetrate to the inner shoots. Although the flowers are too large to be of any value on a bonsai, some people like them. To induce flowering, treat as crab apples (*see* p. 124).

Wire in autumn or late winter. Take care — the bark is soft and can be damaged easily.

Soil and repotting

Repot every two or three years when roots fill the pot. Use an ericaceous and well-drained potting mix.

Getting started

- Buy an established bonsai.
- Sow seeds in pots in late winter or early spring and place in a cold frame.

Styrax japonicus
Japanese snowball

Sometimes sold as *Styrax japonicum* or *Styrax japonica*, this native of China, Korea and Japan is a small and graceful deciduous tree. It grows often in temperate climates, but in cold areas late spring frosts may damage the flower buds and young shoots. In early summer it bears masses of bell-shaped, fragrant white flowers with yellow stamens.

Looking after your plant

Position and temperature

During summer place your plant outdoors in a bright, wind-sheltered position. You can take it indoors in early summer, however, when it is flowering. In winter place it in a cool bright position; avoid high temperatures.

Watering and misting

During summer keep the soil moist, especially when the plant is flowering. In winter reduce the amount of water and keep the soil barely moist. Mist spray the leaves in summer, but not when they are in strong direct sunlight.

Feeding

From mid-spring to late summer, feed your plant every two or three weeks with a weak liquid fertilizer. Do not feed the plant in winter.

Pruning and training

You can prune your plant at any time of the year, but preferably after the flowers fade. You can wire your plants immediately after the flowers fade.

Soil and repotting

Use well-drained potting mix with extra-sharp sand and grit. Repot your plant every two or three years, in early spring before growth begins.

Styles to consider

Getting started

- Buy an established indoor bonsai.
- Buy a small potted plant and modify it into an indoor bonsai (*see* pp. 28–35).
- Sow seeds in autumn in pots. Place the pots in a cold frame (*see* pp. 19–21 and 27).
- In midsummer take 3-inch (7.5 cm) half-ripe cuttings with heels. Insert the cuttings in pots in equal parts moist peat and sharp sand. Place the pots in a cold frame (*see* pp. 26–28).

Styles to consider

Getting started

- Buy an established indoor bonsai.
- Buy a small potted plant from a garden center and modify it into an indoor bonsai (*see* pp. 28–35).
- In autumn sow seeds in pots. Place the pots in a cold frame (*see* pp. 19–21 and 27).

Ulmus parvifolia
Chinese elm

Lacebark elm

Earlier known as *Ulmus chinensis*, this graceful semi-evergreen tree from China, Korea and Japan is hardy. The small green leaves are leathery and glossy, and still present halfway through winter. The smooth bark is dark green and, with age, becomes slightly furrowed. *Ulmus parvifolia* flowers in early and mid-autumn, but the flowers are seldom seen on indoor bonsai, if at all. There are several attractive variegated miniature and cork-bark forms of *Ulmus parvifolia*.

Looking after your plant

Position and temperature

In summer place your plant outdoors in a sunny, wind-sheltered area. In winter place it in an unheated room in good light. Ensure the room remains cool throughout winter.

Watering and misting

During summer keep the soil moist, but not saturated. In winter, especially after the leaves have fallen, reduce the amount of water given and keep the soil barely moist. Mist spray the foliage during summer.

Feeding

From early spring to early or mid-autumn, feed your plant at two or three-week intervals with a weak liquid fertilizer. In winter, do not feed your plant.

Pruning and training

Prune young plants when their shoots are 3–4 inches (7.5–10 cm) long, cutting them back to their leaf joints. Older plants can be pruned at an earlier growth stage. You can wire the plant, but this is not advised as the bark can be easily damaged at this stage.

Soil and repotting

Use well-drained potting mix. You only need to repot every three or four years in early spring when the roots fill the container.

Wisteria spp.
Wisteria

Both *Wisteria chinensis* (Chinese wisteria) and *Wisteria floribunda* (Japanese wisteria) are grown as bonsai. They are vigorous deciduous climbers. The leaves are formed of many mid to dark green leaflets. During late spring and early summer they have long drooping clusters of richly fragrant mauve or violet-blue flowers. There are also white-flowered forms.

Looking after your plant

Position and temperature

During summer position the bonsai in good light. In winter place it under a slatted screen to protect it from cold winds and frost.

Watering

Water copiously in spring and summer, and keep soil moist — but not saturated — in the winter months.

Feeding

Feed with a weak liquid fertilizer every 10 to 14 days from when flowering ceases until midsummer; later, every two or three weeks from early to late autumn. Do not feed during winter.

Pruning and training

Cut back your plant to a basic framework of branches immediately after flowering, and allow free growth of all the shoots for as long as possible. After that, cut all long shoots back to two or three buds, and thin out the crowded areas. Repeat as often as necessary during the growing season. Flower buds will begin to form on the stubs of the most recently pruned shoots.

Wire in autumn, after pruning. Little wiring should be needed, since whatever shaping is necessary can be achieved by pruning.

Soil and repotting

Repot your bonsai every two to four years, when roots fill the pot and after the flowers have faded. Ensure the potting mix is well drained.

Styles to consider

Getting started

- Buy an established bonsai.
- Take heel cuttings from the current season's shoots in later summer; insert in equal parts moist peat and sharp sand; place in a heated propagating frame.

Styles to consider

Getting started

✄ Buy an established bonsai.
✄ Sow seeds in pots in late winter or early spring and place in a cold frame.

Zelkova serrata
Japanese elm

Japanese gray-bark elm, Japanese zelkova, saw-leaf zelkova

This hardy deciduous tree has smooth gray bark and dark green leaves, which are tapered oval to lance shaped with serrated edges. In autumn they change color from crimson and bronze to orange and yellow. Even when the branches are bare in winter, the fine twigs of the branches are an attractive feature of the tree.

Looking after your plant

Position and temperature

During summer shelter the plant from strong direct sunlight. In winter position it under a slatted screen to protect it from cold winds and frost.

Watering

Water daily in summer and keep soil moist in winter. Do not overwater at any time.

Feeding

Feed generously while the twigs are developing, and sparingly when the tree is fully formed.

Pruning and training

Prune branches during autumn or late winter, and shoots as necessary throughout the summer. Cut shoots back to one or two leaves.

Wire at any time. Branches are supple and will set in position quite quickly in the spring and summer.

Soil and repotting

Repot every two or three years. It is best to use Japanese Akadama soil or a mixture of 70 percent coarse organic matter and 30 percent grit.

Other indoor bonsai to consider

Bonsai enthusiasts are always experimenting with houseplants to see if they are able to be converted to indoor bonsai. Houseplants with small leaves are easy to train and prune, and can be adapted easily to miniature shapes and stances. If you are interested in taking the cultivation of indoor bonsai to an advanced level, experiment with the list of houseplants on the following pages. If you have a houseplant with fairly large leaves not listed here, leaf prune it repeatedly — this will reduce its leaf size. Plants from the *Ficus* genus are particularly suited to this (see pp. 28–35). Joining a local indoor bonsai society is another way to get further information about plants suitable for indoor bonsai and styles to suit them.

Acacia baileyana
(Cootamundra wattle, golden mimosa)
A small evergreen shrub with pairs of narrow leaflets and fragrant yellow flowers.

Acacia dealbata
(Mimosa, silver wattle)
An evergreen tree that bears small silver-green leaves in neat rows on opposite sides of its branches.

Adenium obesum
(Desert rose, Impala lily, Kudu lily, mock azalea, Sabi star)
A succulent shrub with large pink flowers.

Albizia julibrissin
(Mimosa tree, pink siris, silk tree)
A deciduous tree that bears pomponlike flowers with threadlike pink stamens.

Ardisia crenata
(Coral berry, spice berry)
An evergreen shrub with pink or white flowers followed by coral-red to scarlet berries.

Ardisia crispa
(Shoebutton, coral ardisia)
An evergreen shrub with dark green leaves, pink flowers and red berries.

Bauhinia x *blakeana*
(Hong Kong orchid tree)
An evergreen shrub with orchidlike mauve to bright red flowers.

Bauhinia punctata syn. *Bauhinia galpinii*
(Nasturtium bauhinia, red bauhinia)
A low-spreading evergreen shrub with lobed leaves and orange or red ruffled flowers.

Bougainvillea x *buttiana* 'Mrs. Butt'
('Mrs. Butt,' paper flower)
A plant that can be deciduous or semi-deciduous. Famed for its rose-crimson flowerlike bracts that later fade to magenta.

Brachychiton rupestris (Sterculia rupestris)
(Bottle tree, narrow-leaved bottle tree, Queensland bottle tree)
An evergreen tree with a bottlelike trunk and roots that store water. It has five to seven slightly lobed dark green leaves on long stalks and, as an indoor bonsai, does not bear flowers.

Bucida buceras
(Black olive)
An evergreen tree with leathery leaves and green-yellow flowers.

Bursera microphylla
(Elephant tree, torote)
A small deciduous tree with clusters of white flowers. With age, the branches become cherry red.

Bursera simaruba
(Gum elemi, gumbo-limbo, West Indian birch)
A deciduous tree which, with age, has lustrous light red to dark red peeling bark.

Calliandra haematocephala

(Red powderpuff)

A shrub with powder-puff pink to red flowers.

Casuarina equisetifolia

(Horsetail tree, mile tree, southsea ironwood)

A large evergreen tree with upright pine needles that grow mainly from the upper sides of the branches.

Citrofortunella microcarpa (Citrus mitis)

(Calamondin, Calamondin orange, Panama orange)

A plant with elliptic shiny leaves with slightly winged leafstalks. The white flowers are highly fragrant.

Citrus sinensis

(Orange, sweet orange)

An evergreen tree well known for its fruits. It has long elliptic-shaped, shiny green leaves that have slightly winged leafstalks.

Coccoloba uvifera

(Jamaican kino, platter leaf, sea grape)

An evergreen shrub that has leathery bright green leaves with yellow-green to red veins, fragrant white flowers and edible grapelike fruits.

Coffea arabica

(Arabian coffee, Arabica coffee, coffee)

A plant with dark glossy green leaves and fragrant white flowers followed by red berries.

Conocarpus erectus

(Buttonwood, buttonwood mangrove)

A prostrate evergreen shrub native to the mangrove swamps of tropical North and South America. It has leaves of different shapes and green flowers.

Cupressus macrocarpa 'Goldcrest'

(Golden Monterey cypress)

An evergreen conifer with beautiful sprays of golden leaves.

Eugenia foetida

(Spanish stopper)

An evergreen shrub that has scaly bark and oval dark green leaves with a characteristic droop at their tips. When young, the leaves are bronze.

Ficus deltoidea var. diversifolia

(Mistletoe fig, mistletoe rubber plant)

An evergreen plant with pear-shaped and leathery dark green leaves with pale green undersides. It bears either yellow or dull red inedible berries.

Ficus neriifolia

(Willow-leaf fig)

A small evergreen tree that is briefly deciduous in early spring with lance-shaped leaves that are first red then green.

Fraxinus uhdei

(Evergreen ash, Shamel ash)

An evergreen shrub with lance-shaped, shiny green leaves.

Fuchsia magellanica

(Hardy fuchsia)

Hardy bushy shrub with pale green leaves and pendulous crimson and purple flowers.

Grevillea robusta

(Silk oak, silky oak)

Evergreen shrub that has pale to dark green leaves and silky hairs.

Haematoxylum campechianum

(Bloodwood tree, campeachy, logwood)

An evergreen tree that has prickly branches, gnarled bark, oval light green leaves and small fragrant yellow flowers. Only grow this plant as an indoor bonsai if you are experienced.

Hibiscus rosa-sinensis

(Blacking plant, China rose, Chinese hibiscus, rose of China)

An evergreen shrub with oval dark green leaves and single deep crimson flowers.

Ixora coccinea

(Burning love, flame of the woods, jungle geranium, red ixora)

A small evergreen shrub with brilliant salmon-red flowers.

Ixora javanica

(Javanese ixora, Red ixora)

An evergreen shrub with clusters of beautiful scarlet flowers (sometimes pink or orange).

Jacaranda mimosifolia

(Green ebony, jacaranda)

A small evergreen shrub with pairs of narrow leaflets and fragrant yellow flowers. It has fernlike pale green leaves on long, slightly cascading stems. It bears blue-purple flowers with white throats. Unfortunately, when grown as an indoor bonsai, it seldom produces flowers.

Myrciaria cauliflora

(Brazilian grape tree)

An evergreen tree with smooth flaking bark, mottled in shades of gray and brown. The lance-shaped light green leaves have smooth unbroken edges. The plant also bears clusters of white flowers followed by round edible fruits in colors from white to purple, but most often from blue to dark purple.

Myrsine africana

(African boxwood, cape myrtle, myrsine)

A small evergreen shrub with narrow pale to dark green leaves.

Pinus halepensis

(Aleppo pine, Jerusalem pine)

An evergreen subtropical conifer. In the wild it has slender light green needles that are 6 inches (15 cm) or longer, but when grown as indoor bonsai they are seldom longer than 2 inches (5 cm). The bark is silver gray and later turns red-brown.

Pinus pinea

(Italian stone pine, stone pine, umbrella pine)

A pine with a dense umbrellalike crown packed with pairs of dark green needles; they are light green when the tree is young. The barks of old trees exhibit orange, red and yellow-brown colors and have deep vertical fissures.

Pistacia terebinthus

(Chian turpentine tree, Cypres turpentine, pistachio)

A deciduous subtropical tree with dark green glossy leaves. The flowers are green, and when grown in native areas, they are followed by small, wrinkled purple-red fruits.

Polyscias fruticosa

(Ming aralia)

A tropical evergreen with pale green leaves that have irregular deeply cut edges. The rough bark on the trunk is mottled and light brown.

Rhapis excelsa

(Bamboo palm, fern rhapis, grand rattan, hemp palm)

A palm with reedlike stems and umbrellalike arrangements of long dark green shiny leaves. It is not fully hardy in temperate climates and makes a distinctive indoor bonsai.

Senna alexandrina

(Alexandrina senna, true senna, Tinnevelly senna)

This plant has many pale green leaflets and yellow tawny flowers.

Senna marilandica

(Wild senna)

This plant has many leaflets with yellow pealike flowers.

Tamarindus indica

(Indian date, tamarind, tamarindo)

A large tropical evergreen tree with small pale green leaves that resemble those of the mimosa. The trunk is brown and appears aged. In the wild the flowers are pale yellow, while the fruits are cinnamon-brown and up to 6 inches (15 cm) long. Do not expect to see these on indoor bonsai.

Glossary

Adult foliage Featured on mature plants. When young, some plants have differently shaped and colored leaves from those that appear later.

Air layering A method of propagation that encourages roots to form on a trunk or branch. The bark is partly cut and moisture-retentive material, such as peat or sphagum moss, is packed around it. After roots form, the rooted part is severed from the parent plant and transferred to a pot.

Annealing A softening process that involves heating up wire until it glows red and then allowing it to cool down slowly. This makes it easier to manipulate when used to train and support bonsai. Although this "softening" can be undertaken in a home workshop, it is safer and easier to buy annealed wire from a nursery or specialist store.

Anodized-aluminium wire A type of wire used to change the shape of a branch or trunk of a bonsai tree. The wire is coated in a protective film created by chemical or eletrolytic processes.

Broom Bonsai style, *see* p. 40.

Bud break When a leaf bud opens and reveals a green top.

Callus Corky, hard tissue that forms over a wound on a plant. Usually results in a raised surface, especially around the edges of the tissue.

Cambium Thin layer of cell tissue found just under the bark that initiates growth.

Cascade Bonsai style, *see* p. 39.

Chattachoochie An ingredient in potting mix, often used in North America. It is hard, non-porous and resembles small pieces of gravel or pebbles, ⅛ inch (3 mm) or slightly more across.

Clasped to a rock Bonsai style, sometimes known as root on rock or clinging to a rock (*see* p. 40).

Cold frame A glazed, wooden or concrete-sided framework that protects small plants from cold, wet weather (*see* p. 27).

Compost A mixture of decomposed grass cuttings and vegetable waste used as an organic soil amendment or as a mulch.

Left: *Flowering indoor bonsai create a feast of color. Take care not to position them in drafts or where they can be knocked over.*

Compost firmer A flat implement with a handle made of a ½–¾ inch (12-18 mm) thick piece of wood, used to level soil surfaces.

Compound leaf A leaf formed of two or more leaflets.

Conifer A member of a group of cone-bearing plants. Some conifers, such as *Taxus baccata* (yew) and *Ginkgo biloba* (maidenhair tree), do not bear cones. Some conifers are evergreen, while others are deciduous.

Crown Upper part of a tree where branches spread out from the trunk. Also the base of the tree where the stem and roots join.

Cultivar A plant produced in cultivation and indicating a "cultivated variety." Earlier, all variations, whether produced naturally in the wild or within cultivation, were known as "varieties." The term "variety" has been used by gardeners for many decades and is still frequently seen in books as well as used in conversation.

Cut leaved A tree or shrub with leaves shaped in segments. Some leaves are cut into a few segments, while others are cut more finely.

Deciduous A plant that loses its leaves at the beginning of its dormant season, usually in autumn or early winter. It produces a fresh array of leaves in spring or early summer. This term usually applies to woody plants such as trees, shrubs and climbers, but also to some conifers.

Dibber A blunt-ended or slightly pointed tool (usually made of wood) used for making holes in soil into which the roots of seedlings or plants are inserted. Dibbers used for the insertion of seedlings are usually 4–5 inches (10–13 cm) long, whereas those used for larger garden plants are about 10 inches (25 cm) long and often have a handle.

Down Fine and soft short hairs found on the leaves and fruits of some plants.

Evergreen A plant that appears to be "ever green," but throughout the year sheds some leaves or needles and produces new ones. A few evergreen plants that are native to warm areas become semi-evergreen, or even lose all of their foliage, when in a colder climate.

Exposed roots Some bonsai are trained to have exposed roots to create an impression of maturity. Not all bonsai subjects are suited to this style.

Face side The side of a bonsai that is more attractive than any other. When displaying a bonsai, ensure that the face side (front) is foremost on display.

Formal upright Bonsai style, *see* p. 38.

Genus A group of plants with similar botanical characteristics. Within a genus there are one or more species, each with their own slightly different characteristics.

Germination The process that occurs within a seed when given adequate moisture, air and warmth. The seed coat ruptures and a seed leaf, or leaves, grow upward toward the light. At the same time, a root develops and grows downward. To most gardeners, however, germination is when they see seed leaves appearing through the surface of the potting mix.

Granite grit A hard non-porous ingredient of potting mix that ensures good aeration and drainage.

Group Bonsai style, *see* p. 41.

Habit The growth nature of a plant, either upright or spreading.

Hardwood cuttings A method of increasing plants whereby a cutting is formed of mature wood taken at the end of the growing season.

Hardy A plant that, in temperate climates, can be left outside during winter. Winter temperatures vary dramatically in North America and a winter hardy plant may not survive in all areas.

Heel A small piece of bark or wood left at the base of a semi-hardwood cutting (also known as a semi-ripe cutting).

Humidity The amount of moisture in the atmosphere. The higher the temperature, the more moisture the air retains.

Indoor bonsai Mainly tropical and subtropical plants grown indoors in colder climates. They are also popular in warm climates. This style of bonsai was known as Chinese bonsai.

Informal upright Bonsai style, *see* p. 38.

Internodal The distance between two leaf joints (nodes).

Juvenile foliage Young leaves; may differ from adult foliage.

Leader Usually refers to the main shoot at the tip or end of a branch. It extends the growth of a plant.

Leaning Bonsai style also known as slanting (*see* p. 39).

Literati Bonsai style, *see* p. 40.

Loam Formed of a mixture of sand, clay, silt and decomposed organic material.

Mist spraying The use of a sprayer to create a fine mist of clean water around plants in order to increase the humidity.

Multitrunk Bonsai style, *see* p. 41.

Needle Modified leaf that is narrow and relatively tough in nature. Usually used to refer to the foliage on most conifers.

Outdoor bonsai Trees and shrubs, including conifers, that are hardy in temperate climates and grown outdoors in pots to create dwarf forms of themselves. This is sometimes known as Japanese bonsai.

Pea shingle Clean shingle, usually formed of pieces $\frac{1}{4}$–$\frac{3}{8}$ inch (6–9 mm) wide. Measurements vary, depending on whether the material is sold in metric or imperial measurements.

Peat Partly decomposed vegetable material, usually acidic, often used in potting mixes. Cutting this material from peat beds, however, destroys the environments of many birds, animals and insects.

Perennial A plant that lives for an indefinite period. Usually applies to woody plants but also to herbaceous perennials, whose stems die in autumn or early winter and are replaced by fresh ones in spring.

Perlite A lightweight material that is added to a potting mix to increase its ability to retain moisture and increase aeration.

Pinching back Using fingertips to remove the tips of young shoots. It increases bushiness and controls the size of a plant.

Pinching out *See* Pinching back.

Pot bound When a plant fills its container with roots and has no room to grow. At this stage, a plant is usually repotted.

Potting mix A mixture of friable loam, sharp sand, peat and fertilizer used for houseplants. Potting mixes for bonsai may also contain grit and crushed rock.

Pricking off When seedlings are initially transferred from where they were raised from seeds into seed trays or individual pots that allow for wide spacing between each seedling.

Pruning The controlled removal, or pinching back, of shoots, leaves and stems to control growth and to shape a plant.

Raft Bonsai style, *see* p. 41.

Repotting Moving a plant that fills its existing pot with roots into a larger container. Alternatively, a plant can be repotted into a pot of the same size by cutting away some of the roots.

Root ball The roots and accompanying soil of a plant grown in a pot or other container.

Root on rock Bonsai style, sometimes known as clinging to a rock (*see* p. 40).

Root over rock Bonsai style, *see* p. 40.

Root pruning Cutting back roots of a pot-bound plant. With bonsai, this is usually done at the same time as repotting.

Seed-starting mix A type of potting mix, usually formed of friable loam, sharp sand and peat, that provides seeds with the essentials for germination.

Semi-cascading Bonsai style, *see* p. 39.

Semi-deciduous Some plants that are normally evergreen in their native habitat may, during winter, lose some or all of their leaves when grown in a cold environment.

Sharp sand Gritty coarse sand, also known as builder's sand. It enables air to enter the soil and excess water to drain rapidly.

Slanting Bonsai style, also known as leaning (*see* p. 39).

Softwood cuttings Method of increasing plants, whereby a cutting is formed from a soft, immature shoot that is inserted into potting mix and exposed to gentle warmth.

Species A group of plants that breed together and have the same characteristics. A species belongs to a genus that can be formed of one or more species. Within a species, there may be cultivars and varieties.

Sphagnum Native to bogs, they are able to retain moisture and are occasionally used in potting mixes.

Stratification A method of helping seeds with hard coats to germinate. Seeds are placed between layers of sand and kept cold, usually for the duration of winter.

Systemic An insecticide or fungicide that enters a plant's tissue and provides protection against pests and diseases.

Tender A plant in a temperate climate that is unable to survive winter outdoors.

Texas grit Used in some potting mixes, especially in North America, to ensure good drainage.

Traditional bonsai Miniature hardy trees, shrubs and conifers grown outdoors and in containers in temperate areas.

Tufa rock Porous, soft, moisture-retentive rock that can be easily worked and shaped for decorative use with some forms of bonsai.

Twin trunk Bonsai style, *see* p. 41.

Variety *See* Cultivar.

Vermiculite A light-weight, micalike material added to soil to improve moisture retention.

Windswept Bonsai style, *see* p. 39.

Wound sealant A proprietary compound that is used to seal pruning cuts. It reduces the loss of sap and aids healing.

Index

Acknowledgments

The publisher would like to thank Carl Morrow for his support and guidance, and his presence at the picture shoots, as well as Rudi Adams, who was a great help in supplying some tools, pots and other equipment for photography.